unnatural ecopoetics

# unnatural ecopoetics

## [ *Unlikely Spaces in Contemporary Poetry* ]

SARAH NOLAN

*Foreword by* Scott Slovic

**UNIVERSITY OF NEVADA PRESS** *Reno & Las Vegas*

University of Nevada Press | Reno, Nevada 89557 USA
www.unpress.nevada.edu
Copyright © 2017 by University of Nevada Press
All rights reserved
Cover design by Trudi Gershinov
Cover photograph by Beau Rogers

Library of Congress Cataloging-in-Publication Data
Names: Nolan, Sarah, 1986– author.
Title: Unnatural ecopoetics : unlikely spaces in contemporary poetry / Sarah Nolan ;
    foreword by Scott Slovic.
Description: Reno : University of Nevada Press, 2017. | Includes bibliographical references
    and index.
Identifiers: LCCN 2016048231 (print) | LCCN 2017004070 (e-book) |
    ISBN 978-1-943859-27-6 (hardback) | ISBN 978-0-87417-468-7 (e-book)
Subjects: LCSH: American poetry—21st century—History and criticism. | American
    poetry—20th century—History and criticism. | Philosophy of nature in literature. |
    Ecocriticism. | Poetics. | Environment (Aesthetics) | Human ecology in literature. |
    Experimental poetry, American—History and criticism. | BISAC: LITERARY CRITICISM /
    Poetry. | LITERARY CRITICISM / American / General.
Classification: LCC PS310.N3 N65 2017 (print) | LCC PS310.N3 (e-book) |
    DDC 811.009/36—dc23
LC record available at https://lccn.loc.gov/2016048231

The paper used in this book meets the requirements of American National Standard for
    Information Sciences—Permanence of Paper for Printed Library Materials,
    ANSI/NISO Z39.48-1992 (R2002).

FIRST PRINTING

Manufactured in the United States of America

*To Jacob, Knox, and Alice*

# Contents

# Foreword

THE APPARENT OXYMORON embedded in Sarah Nolan's phrase "unnatural ecopoetics" points to the latest trend in the environmental humanities, which obliterates the naive traditional idea that there is a separate "nature" out there, somehow environing human experience and human constructions.

This project builds deliberately and respectfully on the traditions of nature-poetry studies and experimental ecopoetics that have developed during the past several decades, paying particular attention to the energetic work in North America that has made ecopoetics a cutting-edge aspect of human-nature theory and environmental textual studies. However, it is important to remember that these are global conversations that have long been intrinsic to the eco-critical project, including Nirmal Selvamony's work in Tamil oikopoetics since the 1980s, Hubert Zapf's theorizing of Kulturökologie in Germany and application of this concept of textual ecosystems to American writing, Lu Shuyuan's studies of Tao Yuanming's meditations on classical Chinese philosophies of self and other through artful parables, Niyi Osundare and Tanure Ojaide's yoking of experimental and traditional language and environmental politics in the context of the Niger Delta, and Julia Fiedorczuk and Gerardo Beltrán's ecopoetic exploration of the "radiant web of meaningful things" in multiple cultural contexts, from seventeenth-century Mexico to twenty-first-century Poland.

The three theoretical pillars of *Unnatural Ecopoetics* are as follows: (1) "ecopoetics" is a hermeneutic tool that applies to language and human cultural expression in general, not only to the specific aesthetic mode known as "poetry"; (2) along the lines of posthumanist and new materialist thought, the boundaries between that-which-is-human and that-which-is-not-human have collapsed into an understanding of the hybrid "naturalcultural" reality we inhabit physically and intellectually; and (3) "self-aware textual space[s]" facilitate our understanding of naturalcultural relationships. Some readers may be confused by the apparent doublespeak in the statement that ecopoetics is not concerned specifically with poetry and the tendency of ecopoetic critics and theorists to focus on poetry. Perhaps this focus simply results from the fact that poetry is a highly "self-aware textual space," indeed one of the most self-aware modes of expression, and thus it is an ideal case study for ecopoetic analysis, although such analysis can also be applied to any other mode of discourse.

I have just returned from an international conference on "ecopoetics" at the University of Perpignan in southern France. Panel topics ranged from imagining islands to the politics of Sammi (indigenous Scandinavians) literature, from postcolonial ecocritical readings of South Asian fiction to studies of agricultural memoirs in the United States. In other words, the scholarly focus was all over the intellectual map. Yes, there were panels on Welsh poetry and the epistemological implications of haiku. But poetry qua poetry was not the sole domain of the meeting.

I have long been at peace with this amorphous concept of ecopoetics, but perhaps this is not the case for all scholars in the field or for readers more generally. I think Sarah Nolan's work, so edgy and so grounded and clear at the same time, will contribute greatly to the understanding of what ecopoetics is and what the field does. Her historical mapping of the discipline is worth the price of the book. Her lucid and energetic readings of important texts by Ammons, Hejinian, Howe, and Goldsmith, among others, are bonuses that exemplify best current practices in ecopoetic analysis. And her adventurous speculations truly chart the future—or several possible futures—of the discipline.

Nolan, a product of the built environments of greater Los Angeles, whose ecopoetic ideas have been tempered by years of living in the Great Basin Desert on the eastern slope of the Sierra Nevada, thoroughly understands the nature-culture continuum, while also recognizing and valuing the meaning of natural forces that exceed and constrain the human. She offers an ecumenical view of what an "environment" is and how "this new era of ecopoetic theory" enables readers to appreciate the materiality of texts and the textuality of the physical world.

—SCOTT SLOVIC

# Acknowledgments

I FIRST BEGAN WORKING on this project as a doctoral student at the University of Nevada, Reno, where I received incredible support from my advisors, especially Scott Slovic and Ann Keniston. They continually challenged me to overcome my own doubts and the various hurdles of academic writing to push this project forward. At Nevada, I also had the benefit of working with Cheryll Glotfelty, Erin James, Michael Branch, Paul Starrs, and John Sagebiel, who pushed me in directions I never would have imagined without their guidance. I owe many thanks to those who supported my preliminary ideas for this project, and particularly to George Hart for introducing me to ecopoetics and encouraging me to explore the field with curiosity and an open mind. My gratitude also goes to Bill Mohr and Tim Caron, who helped me explore my early ideas on ecopoetics at California State University, Long Beach.

I have been extremely fortunate to enjoy the friendship and intellectual stimulation of all of my colleagues in the Literature and Environment program at Nevada, especially Will Lombardi, Kyle Bladow, Andy Ross, Sylvan Goldberg, and Tom Hertweck. I also offer my sincerest thanks to my former classmate Beau Rogers for taking the gorgeous photograph of Los Angeles that appears on the front cover.

My appreciation goes out to my mother, Johanna Nolan, for her lifelong support and ongoing encouragement, and to Knox and Alice, for motivating me to always be at my best. Thanks to Jennifer, Kieran, and David for helping me reach a place where I could complete this project. My gratitude extends to my father, Myles Nolan, who I know would have been proud to see this book come to life. Finally, I owe my sincerest thanks to Jacob Harmon, who not only gives me his support and love every day, but also inspires me to be the best scholar, mother, and friend that I can be.

unnatural
ecopoetics

# The Unlikely Environments of Ecopoetics

*It's my lunch hour, so I go*
*for a walk among the hum-colored*
*cabs. First, down the sidewalk*
*where laborers feed their dirty*
*glistening torsos sandwiches*
*and Coca-Cola, with yellow helmets*
*on. They protect them from falling*
*bricks, I guess. Then onto the*
*avenue where skirts are flipping*
*above heels and blow up over*
*grates. The sun is hot, but the*
*cabs stir up the air. I look*
*at bargains in wristwatches. There*
*are cats playing in sawdust.*

—FRANK O'HARA, from "A Step Away from Them"

IN HIS 1964 POEM "A Step Away from Them," Frank O'Hara poeticizes the banal experience of his lunch hour in an urban environment.[1] For the speaker, the walk brings encounters with the mundane happenings of the city, including everything from "hum-colored / cabs" to workers drinking "Coca-Cola." The poem's speaker engages with the wholly constructed and intensely cultural environment in which he walks and reveals the environmentality of the urban space. The setting of the poem is almost entirely unnatural in its lack of traditional images of the natural world, save a momentary reference to "[t]he sun," yet the space is familiar, homely, and even a natural home to the speaker, who portrays the urban space in the comfortable and familiar rhythm of everyday speech, an informality that is reflected in the poem's free verse. The poem's expression of everyday life in the contemporary city occurs through images of lived experience, including material and culturally significant objects that are man-made, industrial, and even frivolous ("the sidewalk," "Coca-Cola," "yellow helmets," "heels," "grates," "cabs," and "wristwatches") along with musings over the poet's real-world personal hardships, extratextual references, and meta-poetic implications of the poem's struggle to express the world.[2] The poem's setting is unnatural, but drawing the experience of that place into a self-aware textual space reveals the naturalcultural elements that shape the poet's encounter with the city. By drawing naturecultures into a text that exposes and even foregrounds the multifaceted environmentality brought on by material and nonmaterial objects, places, thoughts, feelings, connections, and histories, the poem's textual space shows that environmental experiences are always natural-cultural and grants the material world agency in shaping that space.

Given its paucity of traditional natural elements and its focus on human cultural objects and personal sentiments, "A Step Away from Them" would not typically be read ecopoetically. However, I present O'Hara's poem as an example of how to read through a critical lens I call "unnatural ecopoetics." Unnatural ecopoetics emerges from Donna Haraway's new materialist concept of "naturecultures," which she explains as "the implosions of the discursive realms of nature and culture,"[3] and builds on material ecocriticism's proposed breakdown of recognizable boundaries between natural and human spaces, objects, thoughts, and agencies (Haraway 2000, 105). Unnatural ecopoetic techniques use open and often extrapoetic forms and self-reflexive commentary on the failures of words to accurately express material reality in order to foreground naturecultures within the distinctly textual space created by the poem, a space where the agentic power of the material and nonmaterial worlds are revealed as equals. I use the term "material" throughout this book as a way of pointing to the breakdown of boundaries between nature and culture, where "material" stands in for all physical objects and places, whether man-made or occurring naturally in the world. "Nonmaterial," on the other hand, refers to the invisible emotional, historical, political, and personal elements that influence the speaker's experience of space and translation of it to the textual space of the poem. The material and nonmaterial come together in a new space—a textual space. Drawing from Edward Soja, the textual space that I identify is a kind of "thirdspace," where the dichotomy between subjective and objective interpretations of materiality breaks down.[4] Textual space is created when a text is forthcoming about its own constructedness and makes those limitations apparent on the page through formal experimentation, extratextual references, or metapoetic commentary. The location of a textual space is fundamental to the critical lens of unnatural ecopoetics because it is within that self-reflexive space that naturecultures can be made visible and influential.

Reading O'Hara's poem through unnatural ecopoetics reveals how the multiple material and nonmaterial elements of experience are exposed on the page. Marking the beginning of what he terms his "'I do this, I do that' poems,"[5] the poet's musing over the material sights and sounds of the city infuses physical space into the speaker's subjective experience of it. Entirely absent of traditional images of wild nature, the poem provides a glimpse of an experience in the world that acknowledges how physical elements are perceived by the human speaker with the influence of cultural, personal, and textual forces. The text complicates the speaker's walk in his material surroundings by integrating his observations with his analysis ("They protect them from falling / bricks, I guess") and referencing extratextual information. Later in the same poem, the speaker refers to three deaths that dramatically affected the poet: "Bunny [Lang] died, then John Latouche, / then Jackson Pollock" (1964, 16). In a similar moment, the final lines reveal a self-reflexivity to the poem that emerges from a connection to the fragmentation and disjointedness of cubist and surrealist styles: "My heart is in my / pocket, it is Poems by Pierre Reverdy" (1964, 17).[6] Referencing Reverdy and his cubist interest in multiple perspectives, the poem's seemingly simple list of events is complicated by other viewpoints, which shape the speaker's experience. "A Step Away from Them" is built on a form of direct transcription of lived experience to the page,[7] in which the speaker moves between his individual observations, encounters, movements, and thoughts in the order in which he encounters them on his walk. The poet's transcription of his encounters and thoughts creates a textual depiction of his naturalcultural environmental experience. Unnatural ecopoetics reveals that despite the lack of natural elements in O'Hara's poem, it meaningfully engages the physical, cultural, and personal elements of environment within its textual space. When pushed further, though, unnatural ecopoetics also reveals that O'Hara's poem attributes agency to the material forces around the speaker by revealing the power of "skirts" to flip and "blow," cabs to "stir up the air," and, later in the poem, for the "sign" of Times Square to "blow smoke" and for "everything" to "honk" (1964, 15–16). By recognizing how nonhuman elements act within the textual space, an unnatural ecopoetic reading emphasizes poetry's unique suitability for identifying how material and nonmaterial elements alike shape real-world experience and thus demonstrates the "distributive agency" sought by material ecocriticism.

I begin with O'Hara for two reasons. First, "A Step Away from Them" exemplifies the variety of ecopoetry that I explore in this book, as this new lens identifies and elucidates understandings of texts that express materiality as naturalcultural; second, O'Hara's poem, although it initially appears to be a simple transcription, foregrounds the gap between lived experience and textual expressions of it by employing unique formal structures and self-reflexive language that reveal its own textuality. Further, my reading of "A Step Away from Them" is indicative of how I am reading the work of A. R. Ammons, Lyn Hejinian, Susan Howe, and Kenneth Goldsmith, four poets who are unlikely choices for most ecopoetic critiques because of the dominance of unnatural elements in their work. However, I argue that despite the lack of traditional nature in the work of these twentieth- and twenty-first-century poets, many of their poems express environmentality more accurately than do poems by their counterparts who are widely considered to be ecopoets. I take the term "environmentality" from Lawrence Buell, who uses it to refer to environmental experiences that are infused with the influence of personal and cultural phenomena.[8] In other words, environmentality encapsulates the interconnections of material and nonmaterial aspects of experience. By accentuating the material and nonmaterial factors of environmentality and stressing the inherent gap between language and reality, the poems in this book present what I identify as an unnatural ecopoetics.

My work on unnatural ecopoetics builds on previous understandings of the term "ecopoetics" and expands its usefulness beyond texts that contain overtly natural images in order to account for contemporary poems that are responding to changes in how space is conceptualized. While conventional definitions of ecopoetics—which arise from the work of John Elder, Leonard Scigaj, J. Scott Bryson, and Jonathan Bate, who present ecopoetics as mimetic and often activist in its sentiments—tie the term to the natural world and envision ecopoetics as accurately as possible through language and form, they do not sufficiently account for technological or social shifts toward fewer physical and natural spaces and to more digital and built sites. In more recent conceptions of the term, however, such a shift is beginning to become more pronounced. My work extends that of Brenda Iijima and Scott Knickerbocker, who are largely responsible for moving conceptions of ecopoetics away from entirely natural environments as they begin to emphasize the ways in which ecopoetics can enhance understandings of poetry on built spaces, often without much connection to traditional ideas of nature. Even these groundbreaking texts, though, tend to temper their engagement with unnatural spaces by bidding toward the minute natural presences in the texts, often a contaminated or fraught natural element in the urban world.

I present the concept of unnatural ecopoetics as an alternative to models that remain tied, however minutely, to traditionally natural features. My unnatural ecopoetic methodology recognizes that environments are complex spaces, composed not only of things but also context, experience, and language. The human experience of a space is partly nonmaterial and utterly subjective, based entirely on the observer's position, memory, aesthetic preference, and attentiveness, while also hinging on material factors of objects, weather, movement, and the presence of other beings. Unnatural ecopoetics recognizes textual spaces that have the flexibility necessary to account for material and nonmaterial elements of experience. While the word "unnatural" often has negative connotations in ecocriticism and seems to participate in the nature/culture binary that the concept of naturecultures rejects, I use the word not disparagingly or to reinvoke a long-refuted binary but instead as a symbol of the state of contemporary life and the scope of new ecopoetic developments. Inspired by an age shaped by urban infrastructure and relentless technological influences, my use of the term "unnatural" recognizes the unlikely environments that arise in late twentieth and early twenty-first-century literature. At the same time, the term recognizes the challenge it presents to readers; battling two decades of conventional literary approaches to environments in texts through which ecocritics searched painstakingly for traces of nature in writing, unnatural ecopoetics seeks to embrace the need to resist that search. By invoking the term "unnatural," despite its potential to perpetuate a long-contested binary in ecocriticism, unnatural ecopoetics demands that readers remain cognizant of environmentality even when they see no trace of traditional nature on the page. In a sense, this new brand of ecopoetics is unnatural in its illegitimacy; it has no claim to an origin in natural sentiments or forms. Its ecological system is markedly human, but an unnatural ecopoetics moves beyond considering only physical natural elements and instead includes all material and nonmaterial aspects of the environment.[9]

The movement away from traditional ideas of nature and toward an acknowledgment of the complex environmentality that is pivotal in unnatural ecopoetics arises not only from recent ecocriticism, which has demonstrated more theoretical interest in environments beyond nature than most work on ecopoetics, but also from theories of the new materialisms, which posit a movement away from restrictive conceptions of nature and the breakdown of identifiable boundaries between the human body and the rest of the world. As my term extends from ecocriticism, Timothy Morton's ideas in *Ecology Without Nature* are of particular relevance to my own shifting of ecopoetics away from rigid conceptions of nature. Morton proposes a theory of "*ambient poetics,* [which is] a materialist way of reading texts with a view to how they encode the literal space of their inscription—if there is such a thing—the spaces between the words, the margins of the page, the physical and social environment of the reader" (2007, 3; emphasis in original).[10] Although Morton is particularly attuned to the reader's influence on the text in a way I am not, my concept of unnatural ecopoetics builds on his push to recognize how text affects form, and moves beyond its limit on the page into the "physical and social" environment around it. Extending Morton, I analyze texts that recognize the profound influence of human culture and subjectivity on environmental experience. In engaging developments in ecocritical theory along with ecopoetic theory, this book reveals that ecopoetics is useful in understanding not only how natural aspects of a space are expressed in text, but also the multiple levels of natural-cultural spaces.

The ideas of unnatural ecopoetics are best suited to contemporary texts because contemporary poets do not live in a world where nature is distinguishable from culture, where language is distinct from literature, or where the digital is decipherable from the real. These categories have broken down with the increasing move toward the city and corresponding corrosion of wild spaces, the rise of the information age, and the prominence of technologies that alter and increase the variety of ways that individuals can experience the world. As such, developments in ecopoetic theory must respond to changes in contemporary poetry. Christopher Arigo identifies the connections between new poetry and new ecopoetic practices when he writes: "much of the ecopoetry being written seems to take place more in the realm of the innovative, as opposed to more mainstream poetries. Perhaps this is because innovative poetries are loci of resistance to mainstream poetic practices (and values) which presumably reflect larger social paradigms" (2008, 3). In order to better account for environmentality within the innovative practices of contemporary poetry, *Unnatural Ecopoetics* extends previous theoretical threads that address how social changes have irreversibly altered conceptions of the "eco," changing the meaning of ecopoetics to reflect the increasingly unnatural state of contemporary life. Specifically, unnatural ecopoetics offers a critical lens that focuses on the methods by which poets express nonmaterial cultural, historical, political, and personal elements of environmental experience along with material objects and spaces through self-reflexive language and experimental forms, which foreground textual spaces where multiple elements are shown to shape environmentality. Following recent trends in ecocritical theory to think of nature as interconnected within other aspects of space and experiences within it, my conceptualization of unnatural ecopoetics focuses on the ways in which individual memory, personal experience, ideology, and the limitations of the senses play a role in how individuals experience material elements of the world and, just as importantly, on how new forms and experimentation with language can work to express these facets of experience. Unnatural ecopoetics helps to solidify understandings of the field and ultimately enhances its usefulness to scholars both within ecocriticism and beyond by demonstrating that the foregrounded influence of naturecultures within the textual space of contemporary experimental poetry can express various agential powers that highlight the influence of both material and nonmaterial forces in human experience.

## ECOPOETICS AND NEW ECOCRITICAL THEORY

Since its inception, the term "ecopoetics" has remained somewhat amorphous and thus difficult to define and apply. Many scholars define the term, but their conceptions of ecopoetics vary widely and are sometimes directly contradictory. The undefined character of the term is clearly summarized in Timothy Clark's 2011 book, *The Cambridge Companion to Literature and the Environment*, when he contends that "the term *ecopoetry* still has an opportunistic feel" and claims that often "'ecopoetry' does just mean work with a vaguely green message" (139–40; emphasis in original). Pointing to popular environmental literary and social trends, many scholars and poets view ecopoetics and ecopoetry as involved in politicized movements to make poetry relevant to current real-world concerns, often without much or any recognition of the theory behind the term "ecopoetics." To some degree, this lack of consensus falls between two terms that are often viewed as synonyms—ecopoetry and ecopoetics. Despite their often interchangeable use throughout ecocritical scholarship, I argue that these terms have followed quite different paths, as "ecopoetry" has come to refer to poetry that engages with environments for the sake of political and social action, while "ecopoetics" is a methodology or theoretical lens that considers the nuances of how environmental experiences are expressed on the page. Even applications of the term "ecopoetics" are diverse; it is sometimes used to describe a poem's engagement in political expressions of problems in the natural environment and other times recognizes how "nature" can be expressed through nontraditional language and forms. Regardless of the variations in its definition, ecopoetics generally tends to involve analyzing how poems move beyond idealized interactions with the physical world and begin to represent nature for its own inherent value and autonomous self.

For two decades, such scholars as John Elder, Jonathan Bate, Leonard Scigaj, Angus Fletcher, Jonathan Skinner, Jed Rasula, J. Scott Bryson, and Scott Knickerbocker, among many others, have wrestled with the definition of ecopoetics. While the definitions of ecopoetics promoted by these scholars have yet to reach any clear consensus, leaving the term vague and difficult to apply,

each conceptualization of the term yields new insights and directions for ecopoetic studies. The concept of ecopoetics began with examinations of the struggles faced by contemporary nature poets; early studies such as John Elder's
*Imagining the Earth: Poetry and the Vision of Nature* (1985) and Jonathan Bate's
*The Song of the Earth* (2000), which brought the term "ecopoetry" into play,
considered the specifics of what makes a poem an ecopoem but did little to distinguish the field from the more general category of nature poetry.[11] As a result,
some scholars use the term "ecopoetry" synonymously with the general term
"nature poetry" and others have defined it as a more theoretical practice.[12]

The conflicting directions of these early definitions are only a sample of the
many disparate directions of ecopoetic theory within the United States.[13] The
common themes in these definitions are that early ecopoetic theory is closely
tied to traditional ideas of nature and is not inclusive of the personal, historical,
political, and technological elements that contribute to environmental experience. In recent ecopoetic theory, though, scholars are reconceptualizing early
ecopoetics to more closely respond to the concerns of contemporary poets,
who engage with new challenges brought on by an increasingly technological,
global, and urban environment. The stark social shifts faced by contemporary
poets demand new modes of examining how environments are expressed poet-
ically. As Ursula Heise writes in *Sense of Place, Sense of Planet: The Environmental Imagination of the Global*, "the future cannot be symmetrical with the
past because economic, demographic, and ecological conditions have changed
in such a way that radical new forms of social organization are required" (2008,
86). As scholars recognize that the world has changed, so too must they conceptualize a change in ecopoetics. It is in the wake of this shift that I offer
unnatural ecopoetics, which accounts for the physical, cultural, technological,
and social shifts that have occurred in the late twentieth and early twenty-first
centuries by acknowledging the breakdown of the nature/culture binary and
emphasizing a textual space where the effect of material and nonmaterial elements of experience can be revealed.

Changes within ecopoetics, which have been coming for some time, are
prominent in recent studies but can be seen even in some early work. Arguably,
the movement toward a new era of ecopoetics began in the pages of *Ecopoetics*, a journal edited by Jonathan Skinner in which definitions of ecopoetry and ecopoetics have been discussed and debated since 2001. Skinner's
editorial statement in volume one reveals that concerns over the applicability of ecopoetics extend back a decade and a half, and his statement establishes the differences between the journal's purpose and contemporaneous
ecopoetic ideas. He writes that "the developing complexity of perception is

technology-induced, but it also arises from our awareness of a web of nearly unquantifiable interrelatedness that increases, ironically, with human fragmentation of that web" (Skinner 2001, 6). Put another way, the more humans attempt to disconnect themselves from the physical world or destroy the "web" of "unquantifiable interrelatedness," the more those inescapable interrelations are revealed. The human individual is always connected to the world in complex and often invisible ways.[14] Skinner's statement demonstrates that some ecopoetic ideas from an earlier era, such as Skinner's own, recognize the complex interrelations of nature and culture along with experimental forms and thus align more closely with what I identify as unnatural ecopoetics, while some contemporary proponents of the field are more concerned with traditional ideas of nature and mimetic forms that seek to express them and thus align with traditional ecopoetic ideas. While there is a great deal of overlap in the development of traditional ecopoetics and ideas that I call "unnatural ecopoetics," theorizing the more recent era of ecopoetics is directly benefited by contemporary ecocritical and new materialist theory. With this new theory, ecopoetics fractures into two camps, the traditional and the unnatural—one rooted in first- and second-wave ecocriticism, the other grounded in third- and fourth-wave ecocriticism.[15] While the development of ecopoetics has not been a chronological process as in the wave metaphor that is used prominently throughout ecocriticism, positioning the term in relation to ecocritical waves emphasizes the theoretical platforms on which ecopoetics has and continues to build. By acknowledging the ways ecopoetics has broken into distinct phases we can maintain the political and social power in traditional work while also allowing for a more theoretically situated branch of ecopoetics.

Unnatural ecopoetics is an outgrowth of third- and fourth-wave ecocriticism because it elucidates poems where naturecultures are made tangible through overtly textual spaces. However, earlier work, as evidenced by Skinner, began the movement of ecopoetics away from natural settings and toward new forms. The trend to revise ecopoetics has gathered considerable support since 2008 with the publication of a variety of new books and articles that reconceptualize traditional ecopoetic ideas for the twenty-first century. In 2008 and 2009, a new and long-awaited issue of Skinner's journal *Ecopoetics* appeared after a four-year hiatus, and Harriet Tarlo guest-edited a special feature on ecopoetics in *How2*, indicating a renewed critical interest in ecopoetic ideas. These volumes provide new forums in which poets and scholars such as Skinner, Forrest Gander, and Jane Sprague imagine new directions in the field.[16]

My work on unnatural ecopoetics relies on the contributions of recent ecopoetic theory that follow the term's resurgence after 2009. Studies like

Brenda Iijima's *The Ecolanguage Reader* (2010)[17] and, even more recently, Scott Knickerbocker's *Ecopoetics: The Language of Nature, the Nature of Language* (2012) specifically call for ecopoetics to rethink the concept of traditional nature and embrace urban, digital, mental, and textual spaces rather than only physical, natural, or green spaces.[18] Unnatural ecopoetic ideas push further than previous studies as they conceptualize environment differently—in a way that breaks down the nature/culture binary and foregrounds textual space to expose the agency of both material and nonmaterial forces.

My call to view naturecultures and their agential power within the textual space of contemporary poetry is directly facilitated by theoretical movements in the new materialisms and material ecocriticism. In ecocriticism, the ways in which environments are conceptualized were altered by the turn toward environmental justice ecocriticism in the mid-2000s, which calls for the inclusion of urban environments and human inhabitants rather than only the pristine wilderness focus of early ecocritical studies, and the movement after 2010 toward material ecocriticism, which recognizes the indistinguishable interconnections of nature and human culture. As such, today ecopoetics is beginning to move away from considering depictions of nature and toward analyzing how experiences of space or environment are directly shaped by both nature and culture. Along with environmental justice ecocriticism, which broadens understandings of the field to include the human subject, the fusion of new materialism with ecocriticism further expands understandings of the environment by positing that the human body is intertwined with his or her environment. For material ecocriticism, which Scott Slovic identifies as the cornerstone of the field's fourth wave, the challenge of viewing the human as intermeshed with the environment demands a more complex discussion of how we perceive that environment.

The ways in which environments and experiences within them are perceived have garnered attention across various disciplines, including such movements as object-oriented ontology (OOO), "thing theory," and material ecocriticism. While all of these movements are grouped under the material turn in literary studies, material ecocriticism is of particular importance to my concept of unnatural ecopoetics because it specifically posits a collapse of boundaries between the human body and material spaces or objects, allowing a breaking down of purely natural or purely cultural environmental experiences. Still, while my work emerges from concepts in material ecocriticism, unnatural ecopoetics differs from it in its acceptance of the gap between language and reality. While material ecocriticism moves away from the social constructedness of words and toward finding discursive practices that can express the "intra-action" of matter and meaning,[19] unnatural ecopoetics seeks to resolve that gap by looking specifically at the textual space of the poem, in which text itself becomes a space where such intra-action is possible. Unnatural ecopoetics focuses on how material elements, ranging from a tree to a taxi cab, intertwine with nonmaterial subjective experiences and express agency through the fore-grounded textual space. In her attempt to define the burgeoning field of mate-rial ecocriticism, Serpil Oppermann suggests that "the natural and the cultural can no longer be thought as dichotomous categories. Rather, we need to theo-rize them together, and analyze their complex relationships in terms of their indivisibility and thus their mutual effect on one another" (Iovino and Opper-mann 2012, 462–63). In other words, through material ecocriticism, scholars rethink subject/object relationships in order to acknowledge and engage with the "other bodies," including natural and human material objects and bodies, in the world on a meaningful level.

Of particular importance to my project is David Abram's insistence that language can emerge from naturecultures. In *The Spell of the Sensuous*, he writes, "Only by affirming the animateness of perceived things do we allow our words to emerge directly from the depths of our ongoing reciprocity with the world" (Abram 1996, 56). In recognizing "the animateness of perceived things," language begins to "emerge" from naturalcultural experience. As with Haraway's breaking down of the boundaries between nature and culture with her term naturecultures, Abram's move to affirm "the animateness of things" makes it impossible to view agency as a uniquely human trait. Rather, as the boundaries between culture and nature dissolve, and the two worlds intertwine and equalize in the textual space, agency distributes beyond the human and into other aspects of the material world. Such sentiments are echoed in object-oriented ontology (OOO), an approach that is perhaps most clearly illustrated by Jane Bennett's concept of "vibrant matter," through which she attempts "to give voice to a vitality intrinsic to materiality, in the process absolving matter from its long history of attachment to automatism or mechanism" (2010, 3). Much like Abram, Bennett centralizes the need to grant agential power to mate-rial objects and recognize their inherent capacities to affect human actions.

As humans acknowledge the agency of nonhuman and even nonliving objects, their conceptions of what environments are become radically altered. The term "environment," for many people, is immediately tied to the natural elements of a physical landscape. However, as material ecocriticism challenges traditional boundaries between the human self and everything seemingly out-side it, environment moves beyond the "nature is over there" mentality and toward a more interconnected vision. The changing image of environment that follows the new materialisms is evident in *Bodily Natures: Science, Environ-ment, and the Material Self*, where Stacy Alaimo observes that "understanding the substance of one's self as interconnected with the wider environment marks a profound shift in subjectivity. As the material self cannot be disentangled from networks that are simultaneously economic, political, cultural, scientific, and substantial, what was once the ostensibly bounded human subject finds herself in a swirling landscape of uncertainty" (2010, 20). Alaimo contends that the human body cannot be viewed as separate from everything that surrounds it; instead it becomes affected and shaped by its environment, thus shifting the traditional power dynamic of humans dominating nature. Material ecocriticism posits that the human body is always engaged with various influences or "networks" that formulate its experience of the world. Humans are integrated into the environments they inhabit rather than simply being observers, thus making everything human inherently environmental.

As ecocriticism and, subsequently, ecopoetics, moves away from a traditional separation of human culture from the physical world and embraces the new materialisms that draw out naturecultures, new types of texts that formally articulate such spaces become relevant. Oppermann claims that texts in this vein "erase the distinction between the discursive and the material, language, and reality" and ultimately show that "discourse and matter are inextricably entangled, and...constitute life's narratives and life itself" (Iovino and Oppermann 2012, 462). Expressing the dissolution of boundaries between word and world demands the figurative abilities of literary texts. Ultimately, in their book-length study of material ecocriticism, Iovino and Oppermann attribute to literature a unique ability to express the agential promise presented by naturecultures when they claim that "literary stories emerge from the intra-action of human creativity and narrative agency of matter" (2014, 8). As scholars like Oppermann and Alaimo, among others, theorize the breakdown of distinct boundaries between the human body and the environment, what is considered "environment" rapidly changes, and, I argue, what constitutes valid poetry for ecopoetics similarly shifts.

The changes that are occurring in ecopoetic theory signal a new era in ecopoetics (while still leaving room for important traditional ecopoetic concerns), which emerges out of an age of urbanization and technologization, and which is conceptualized through a theoretical lens that is contemporaneous with the poetry of this period. *Unnatural Ecopoetics* presents a term that is significantly different from traditional understandings of the field and not only investigates how this new iteration of the term grows from recent ecopoetic theory but also proposes its continued expansion toward increasingly unlikely poetic spaces.

## UNNATURAL ECOPOETICS

The distinctions between unnatural ecopoetics and traditional conceptions of the term are evident in the "Editor's Preface" to *The Ecopoetry Anthology*, where Ann Fisher-Wirth observes that "ecological poetry is...willing to engage with, even play with, postmodern and poststructuralist theories associated with L=A=N=G=U=A=G=E poetry[20] and the avant garde.... [But] the risks for ecological poetry include hyperintellectualism and emotional distance or detachment" (Fisher-Wirth and Street 2013, xxix). Fisher-Wirth rightly points out the ways in which new ecopoetic theories engage with postmodernism and poststructuralism as represented by developments in the journal *Ecopoetics*, and, among others, Iijima's and Knickerbocker's books. The emerging engagement of ecopoetic critique with language poetry demonstrates the field's interest in the words themselves rather than just their meanings. Yet, this definition disparages the "hyperintellectualism" of radical experimentation that accompanies such movements. My departure from Fisher-Wirth's definition comes in suggesting that the movement of unnatural ecopoetics toward "distance or detachment" brought on by self-reflexive language and experimental forms is precisely what allows this new era of ecopoetics to express the type of natural-cultural environment that was always removed from traditional ecopoetics. In this sense, by embracing its own textuality and demanding that the reader remain aware of the "distance" between the text and materiality, unnatural ecopoetics exposes how invisible and subjective aspects of environmental experience are intertwined with the material space. By moving into the language and engaging textual space, unnatural ecopoetics strives to become truly expressive of the multifaceted material and nonmaterial elements that compose environments. In this sense, unnatural ecopoetics is centered on preserving the complexity in environments by emphasizing the many elements that compose them.

Unnatural ecopoetics displays two continually evolving characteristics that distinguish it from first-wave conceptions of ecopoetics: first, it acknowledges and engages with unnatural physical environments and the various material and nonmaterial elements that constitute them; second, it foregrounds the limitations of language and form. Recent ecopoetic theory embraces concepts from language poetry,[21] which identify language as something meaningful in itself and thus foreground the textual space. Knickerbocker, whose work edges toward unnatural ecopoetics, articulates this shift when he writes that

> [eco]poems undo simple oppositions between humans and nature;
> sensuous poesis operates from the assumption that humans (and their
> tools, including language) are both distinct and inseparable from the
> rest of nature. Rather than attempt to erase the artifice of their own
> poems (to make them seem more natural and supposedly, then, closer
> to nature), the poets in this book unapologetically embrace artifice—
> not for its own sake, but as a way to relate meaningfully to the natural
> world. Indeed for them, artifice *is* natural. (Knickerbocker 2012, 2)

Knickerbocker observes that words are inherently artificial and unable to
express the physical space accurately. He contends that ecopoetry deals with
the problems of language by embracing and foregrounding the "artifice" of the
text. When Knickerbocker's book is put alongside a somewhat similar earlier
study, Scigaj's *Sustainable Poetry*, the distinction between traditional ecopoetics
and the movement in recent ecopoetic theory toward what I call unnatural
ecopoetics becomes evident. Initially, Knickerbocker's point seems to mirror
Scigaj's observation that "within ecopoetry...language is often foregrounded
only to reveal its limitations, and this is accomplished in such a way that the
reader's gaze is thrust beyond language back into the less limited world that
language refers to" (Scigaj 1999, 38). When the two passages are compared,
it is clear that both see ecopoets as engaging with the artificiality of language
or, put another way, the reality that word and world are unequal. For Scigaj,
though, foregrounding the boundaries of language allows the reader to look
past its artificiality to the physical space behind it; Knickerbocker, on the other
hand, observes that "artifice is natural," implying that the words themselves are
tangible, meaningful, and even "natural." While traditional ecopoetics, as represented by Scigaj, engages with text in order to get at the physical space, unnatural ecopoetics builds on Knickerbocker's push toward artifice by embracing
text as space and flaunting its textuality.

Ecopoetics can move toward the type of self-awareness that Knickerbocker proposes only by employing nontraditional forms and self-reflexive
language, which distance the text from direct expressions of reality and exaggerate its inevitable subjectivity. In recent scholarship on ecopoetics, though,
the experimentalism of much contemporary poetry is questioned as a viable
application of the ecopoetic lens. Jill Magi contends in "Ecopoetics and the
Adversarial Consciousness: Challenges to Nature Writing, Environmentalism,
and Notions of Individual Agency" that "though ecopoetics might be grounded
in literary experimentalism, whose traditions have included a deep skepticism
of traditional grammar, narratives, and 'telling,' I believe an ecopoetic stance
may be wary of the fixity of that aesthetic and conceptual position" (2010, 249).

She claims that reworking language is ineffective because such moves are them-selves outdated. Even "experimentalism" must be rethought and redeployed to escape the "fixity" that has been engrained within it. Thus, while Magi implies that ecopoetry is a type of literary experimentalism that must constantly re-invent itself to escape "fixity," Knickerbocker views ecopoetry as something conscious and accepting of its own limitations in expressing lived experience. In my conception of unnatural ecopoetics, both literary experimentalism and self-awareness emerge as tools by which the poem recognizes its own medium. In its awareness of its own limitations, unnatural ecopoetics identifies textual spaces in which naturecultures are distinctly present and where the material world can claim the agency it is denied in traditional ecopoetics through its influence on the textual space.[22]

The poets in this book all engage with unnatural physical environments and emphasize the mediated nature of experiences with the material world through investigations into the limitations of language. Their work acknowl-edges the subjectivity of experience and the subsequent interrelation of nat-ural and cultural forces within experience, a fusion that is expressed within the textual spaces of their poems. The four chapters build on one another as they work from the more literal setting of A. R. Ammons's garbage heap to the figurative space of Goldsmith's found radio reports. As the chapters work chronologically forward,[23] they establish that the uncovering of material and nonmaterial elements of experience in more figurative settings display more clearly the agential power of material elements. While the first chapter demon-strates an intertwining of nature and culture on a physical level through the setting of the trash heap, a place of literal mingling of nature and culture, the second chapter translates that naturalcultural fusion to experiences of physi-cal space by emphasizing the role of subjectivity and nonmaterial influences on human encounters with the environment. The naturalcultural reality of both setting and experience are foundational to chapter 3, in which the influences of nature and culture are central to conceptualizations of language and its abil-ity to express lived experience. Once the influence of naturalcultural forces on language is recognized, chapter 4 propels that fusion into the form of con-ceptual poetry, which captures the naturalcultural experience within a delib-erately pronounced textual space. I work through one new aspect of unnat-ural ecopoetics in each chapter, and culminate with a conclusion that points toward new deployments for the unnatural ecopoetic lens in texts that com-bine all four characteristics.

Chapter 1, "The Material Speaks in A. R. Ammons's *Garbage*," proposes that unnatural ecopoetics allows for renewed interest in a poet who is most often thought of as a traditional ecopoet. In this chapter, I contend that despite the naturalcultural elements of Ammons's later work, it often continues to be read through the lens of traditional ecopoetics. While many scholars attribute the poet's late work to the same methodology as his early poems, such as his famous "Corsons Inlet,"[24] I argue that interpretations of Ammons's late poetry as analogous to his early work are challenged by the introduction of unnatural ecopoetics, which emphasizes his movement away from mimesis and toward spaces that complicate the nature/culture binary in his late work.[25] This chapter acknowledges naturalcultural intersections and deepens understandings of the text's poetics by proposing that in *Garbage*, the poet foregrounds the new naturalcultural objects that emerge from the filth of the trash heap. Through the lens of unnatural ecopoetics readers can look at Ammons, a poet whose early work easily aligns with traditional ecopoetics in its mimetic language and form, and finally understand how the naturalcultural union in his later work is ultimately tied to material and textual reconstitutions and reemergences.

Chapter 2, "From Perception to Text in Lyn Hejinian's *My Life*," considers Lyn Hejinian's poetry as an examination of how formal structure and self-reflexivity reveal the naturalcultural elements that constitute experience. Written in prose poetry, without punctuation, and in the unpredictable order of the human mind's wanderings, *My Life* embodies experience in all of its complications and multiplicities. Since Hejinian's work rarely considers environmental themes and is highly involved in anthropocentric concerns, two traits that are not typical of traditional ecopoetics, critics regularly place her poetry squarely within the realm of language poetry for her acknowledgment of language as a construction and never in terms of ecopoetry. However, unnatural ecopoetics reveals that Hejinian's use of language poetry's methods is central to her acknowledgment that experience is naturalcultural. Although nature is not prominent in *My Life*, Hejinian's poetry engages with naturecultures by integrating facets of the personal, material, and textual into a single textual space. For Hejinian, this attempt to express the complex multiplicity and diversity of an environmental experience in text is accomplished through explorations in forms that can most closely preserve the multifaceted and divergent facets of lived experience and metapoetic inquiries into how language itself can express it. By not reducing the lived moment to a single perspective, Hejinian's work attempts to maintain the complex, multidirectional, confusing, and unrelated features of one's experience in a particular place and time while simultaneously granting agency to the material. Through a search for language that accurately conveys the immediate sensations and multiplicity of experience and her application of that search within her own poetic form, Hejinian unknowingly participates in a fundamental quest of unnatural ecopoetics—to acknowledge naturecultures and integrate them into a poem that foregrounds its own textual space.

Chapter 3, "Toward Textual Space in Susan Howe's *The Midnight*," engages with a highly experimental contemporary poem that seamlessly connects cultural data with personal reflection and physical environment. Examining the fusion of these various elements within the book allows for a better understanding of how unnatural ecopoetics engages just as much with the cultural influences of Howe's Irish heritage and family history as it does with natural ones. *The Midnight* (2003) brings together various aspects of culture, history, environment, and genealogy in a collage that highlights middle spaces, including the space between the poetry and prose sections of the book, which are themselves new environments for ecopoetic critique. In these spaces, various cultural artifacts intermingle—the original poetry, found text, historical data, images, and metapoetic commentary on how language functions. Howe explains that in this book she is "assembling materials for a recurrent return somewhere. Familiar sound textures, deliverances, vagabond quotations, preservations, wilderness shrubs, little resuscitated patterns. Historical or miraculous. Thousands of correlations have to be sliced and spliced" (2003, 85). In this sense, the poem is a fusion of the innumerable aspects of experience, including material and nonmaterial elements. *The Midnight* brings these elements together as it engages in formal and linguistic inquiries into the ability of language to express physical experience as it is infused with culture. Reading *The Midnight* through the lens of unnatural ecopoetics reveals that the poet's interest in history and culture inform her experiences of environments and shape her textual space.[26] It is by engaging with this history and foregrounding its presence that Howe's integration of found text along with personal response and poetic inquiry creates a textual space derived from lived experience. Reading Howe's book through unnatural ecopoetics enhances our understanding of the project, and reveals the diverse applicability of this new branch of ecopoetic theory. Through this lens, Howe—a foundational contemporary poet who, like Hejinian, is often associated with language poetry but has remained outside the scope of ecopoetics and of ecocriticism generally—can finally be fully recognized for her interest in how environments are expressed.

Chapter 4, "The Agency of Found Text in Kenneth Goldsmith's *Seven American Deaths and Disasters*," considers Goldsmith's conceptual poetry[27] through the lens of unnatural ecopoetics by considering its primary focus on unnatural experiences, objects, or events, and its simultaneous examination of how specific real-world moments are experienced both personally and culturally through broadcasts that shape public sentiment and the broadcasters who deliver the message. In *Uncreative Writing: Managing Language in the Digital Age* (2011), Goldsmith argues that "by taking our city's physical geography and overlaying it with *psychogeography*—a technique of mapping the psychic and emotional flows of a city instead of its rational street grids—we become more sensitive to our surroundings.... Geography, then—that most concrete of propositions to which we are bound—is reconfigurable and customizable through the imagination" (2011, 37). Here, Goldsmith contends that encounters with environments are more meaningful when viewed through a lens that captures both geography and individual experience. In *Seven American Deaths and Disasters* Goldsmith puts this philosophy into practice. Transcribing radio and television reports of a number of recent national deaths and disasters, Goldsmith creates a poetic expression of these lived experiences by overlaying them with the various cultural depictions that arose with the events themselves. In found poems like Goldsmith's, language is extracted directly from the lived experience—cultural, digital, natural, and political. As Goldsmith transcribes reports from particular experiences in the world, he expresses those moments without further translating them through the poet's own language, but instead takes cultural artifacts and puts them together on paper in order to illustrate the complex narratives that constructed that moment. In this way, the found poetry that is represented by Goldsmith's work, although entirely unnatural, can still be read ecopoetically. This is the final chapter because Goldsmith's book displays the ways in which the kind of recycling of language apparent in early iterations of unnatural ecopoetics, such as Ammons's *Garbage*, is reconceptualized and extended in new forms and in response to the social, environmental, and technological realities at hand. By reconstituting the very cultural artifacts that shape everyday human experiences in the world—news reports, snippets of information, photographs, and uncontextualized information that we are constantly exposed to through our highly digitized lives—Goldsmith creates textual environments that are literally composed of experiences.

As this book identifies the relevance of unnatural ecopoetics in a variety of unlikely poetic spaces, its conclusion points to further applications and developments for ecopoetic theory. Since the prefix *eco-* is typically used in modern culture as a reference to the environmental movement, the deployment of the term "ecopoetics" in relation to poems that are seemingly absent of nature is somewhat unusual. However, the shift toward unnatural ecopoetics is closely aligned with changes that have already taken place in ecocriticism more generally. As new materialist ideas ask us to question where we draw the line between nature and culture, the concept of a purely natural environment is becoming increasingly fictional. Rather, environments are revealed as all around us—ranging from our own bodies to the digital and textual places that we construct. As ecopoetics begins to engage with these new ideas and expands its boundaries to include less traditional understandings of environment, it becomes more widely applicable. The book's conclusion, "The Future of Ecopoetics in New Poetries and New Spaces," demonstrates that with the shift toward unnatural ecopoetics, biological art like Christian Bök's poem *The Xenotext*, and visual art, including the mixed media work of Patrick Haemmerlein and Robert Grenier's drawn poems, become reasonable texts to read ecopoetically, thus opening the field to new applications and thus new understandings of how individuals conceive of and interact with their environments. These radically divergent texts are useful here because, while unconventional, they all imagine a text as malleable to the moment, evolving alongside experience. Once ecopoetics has the flexibility to recognize diverse expressions of naturecultures, it becomes capable of considering how a wide array of texts employ and engage with environment. In doing so, it highlights the various and often underrepresented ways in which individuals encounter and engage with the world, thus revealing that even unnatural spaces are shaped by material and nonmaterial forces in the environmental experience.

## NOTES

1. "A Step Away from Them" appears in O'Hara's *Lunch Poems*.

2. The speaker's contemplation of death occurs later in the poem when he states: "First / Bunny died, then John Latouche, / then Jackson Pollock." Brad Gooch comments in *City Poet: The Life and Times of Frank O'Hara* that "A Step Away from Them" is the first poem O'Hara wrote after the death of these three famous friends and acquaintances, all of whom died within a short period of time (1993, 285–87). O'Hara's reflections on death occur in relation to their physical demise but also through his consideration of death in relation to the physical environment around him. Later in the poem, he reflects on "the Manhattan Storage Warehouse, / which they'll soon tear down," implying a connection between the physical death of people and the figurative death that occurs constantly within the city. The city is a place of change and adaptation, something always responding to its surroundings. By connecting the physical and the figurative conceptions of death in these later lines, the poet reveals that the unnatural environment of the city is deeply in tune with life, both human and natural.

3. Haraway introduces the term "naturecultures" in *How Like a Leaf: An Interview with Thyrza Nichols Goodeve* (1998).

4. In *Thirdspace: Journeys to Los Angeles and Other Real-and-Imagined Places*, Edward W. Soja outlines the ideas of "firstspace," which is purely material, and "secondspace," which positions "the idealist versus the materialist, the subjective versus the objective interpretation" (1996, 75, 78). In response to these, Soja outlines the concept of "thirdspace," where subjective and objective experience, "structure and agency, mind and body, consciousness and the unconscious," all come together (56–57).

5. O'Hara introduces this term in his poem "Getting Up Ahead of Someone (Sun)" (O'Hara 1971, 341).

6. Reverdy is an early twentieth-century poet who is closely associated with cubist and surrealist artistic movements.

7. In *City Poet: The Life and Times of Frank O'Hara*, Brad Gooch writes that the poem "follows O'Hara in handheld camera fashion, wearing his trademark seersucker Brooks Brothers jacket with a volume of poems by Pierre Reverdy stuck in its pocket, as he heads on his lunch hour west and then downtown from the Museum, past construction sites on Sixth Avenue, through Times Square where he stops for a cheeseburger and a glass of papaya juice beneath the Chesterfield billboard with blowing smoke, and then back uptown to work. In the writing of the poem O'Hara left a record for history of the sensations of a sensitive and sophisticated man in the middle of the twentieth century walking through what was considered by some the capital of the globe" (1993, 288).

8. In *The Future of Environmental Criticism*, Buell proposes that critics move away from conceptions of environment as separate from human culture and instead "think inclusively of environmentality as a property of any text—to maintain that all human artifacts bear such traces, and at several stages: in the composition, the embodiment, and the reception" (2005, 25).

9. I use the word "ecological" as it is defined by the *Oxford English Dictionary*: "Of, relating to, or involving the interrelationships between living organisms and their environment."

10. Morton's theory of "ambient poetics" rightly prompts ecocritics to acknowledge the mediated reality of language and accounts for the artificiality of writing's medium by recognizing the page itself. However, for Morton, ambient poetics is fleeting and can exist only for a passing moment (Morton 2007, 50–51). Unnatural ecopoetics, while growing from Morton's ideas, differs significantly from his "ambient poetics" because it identifies the environmentality at the core of contemporary poems, which does not diminish with the moment but presents a new framework for textual expression of environmental experience that is fully imbued with culture, subjectivity, and physical reality simultaneously.

11. Nature poetry involves a kind of Romantic engagement with the natural world. In *The Ecopoetry Anthology*, Ann Fisher-Wirth and Laura-Gray Street explain that nature poetry is "shaped by romanticism and American transcendentalism [and] often mediates on an encounter between the human subject and something in the other-than-human world that reveals an aspect of the meaning of life. But not all nature poetry is environmental or ecological poetry, and not all nature poetry evinces the accurate and unsentimental awareness of the natural world that is a sine qua non of ecopoetry" (2013, xxviii). Terry Gifford provides an insightful ecocritical examination of nature poetry in *Green Voices: Understanding Contemporary Nature Poetry* (1995).

12. The disparity in existing definitions is apparent in early landmark texts on ecopoetics. Leonard Scigaj, for instance, explains in *Sustainable Poetry: Four American Ecopoets* that ecopoets "record moments of nondualistic inhabitation in specific places where the experience occurs only when the noise of human ratiocination, including the fabrications of language, has been silenced" (1999, 8). In short, Scigaj views ecopoetics as a recording of oneness between a human and a specific place in nature, in which reason, language, thought, and even self are "silenced." In this sense, Scigaj envisions the ecopoem as a place in which a pure moment in nature is preserved. J. Scott Bryson, on the other hand, views ecopoetics as overtly political. In *Ecopoetry: A Critical Introduction*, he argues that ecopoetics involves "an intense skepticism concerning hyperrationality, a skepticism that usually leads to an indictment of an overtechnologized world and a warning concerning the very real potential for ecological catastrophe" (Bryson 2002, 5–6). While Scigaj argues that ecopoetics is primarily about expressing a pure experience, Bryson contends that it is a mode of activism.

13. Although ecopoetics is widely known in the United States as I have described, there are many scholars employing and theorizing the term in other parts of the world, including Chad Weidner, Franca Bellarsi, and Nirmal Selvamony.

14. In his article "Seeking a Center for Ecopoetics," John Linstrom similarly calls for eco-poetics to acknowledge the complexities in perception and representation. He writes: "Any good ecopoetics earnestly seeking to represent nature must recognize the superfluity of human imagination in and against nature and must constantly push the envelope by exploding false walls between human and nonhuman, it must also take into account the role that humans possess as a species uniquely able to empathize with other species and in a unique position of influence over the habitability of the planet" (Linstrom 2011, par. 28). Like many scholars, Linstrom maintains a connection between political activism and ecopoetry.

15. Lawrence Buell describes the first two waves of ecocriticism in *The Future of Environmental Criticism*. He writes: "For first-wave ecocriticism, 'environment' effectively meant 'natural environment.... Second-wave ecocriticism has tended to question organicist models of conceiving both environment and environmentalism" (Buell 2005, 21–22). The second wave brought with it a new interest in urban space, a movement away from pure wilderness, and a recognition of the role that human beings play in environments. In 2010, Scott Slovic and Joni Adamson identified what they call a third wave in ecocriticism, which is increasingly interested in international approaches and begins to consider the interrelatedness of nature and culture. Slovic took up this argument in more depth in "The Third Wave of Ecocriticism: North American Reflections on the Current Phase of the Discipline" (2010). In 2012, he proposed the continued evolution of the field by presenting the concept of a fourth-wave ecocriticism. He writes: "It now seems to me, as we near the end of 2012, that the material turn in ecocriticism is broadening to the extent that it may well represent a new 'fourth wave of ecocriticism'" (Slovic 2012, 619).

16. In "Ecopoetics: Drawing on Calfskin Vellum," Jane Sprague insightfully points out one of the tensions of changing ecopoetic theory: "I hope to challenge and likewise complicate/critique ideas of ecopoetics as a genre. I resist ecopoetics. And definitions of ecopoetics" (2008, 1). Sprague's resistance to definitions of ecopoetics is typical, but it is important to note that it also exacerbates disjunction in conceptions of the term. Without a theoretically rooted methodology, ecopoetics remains so malleable that it is difficult to positively identify. Ecopoetics's resistance to theory, in fact, is reminiscent of ecocriticism's own distaste for theory in its early days, which was overturned by a need for universal methodology.

17. Iijima's collection demonstrates the disconnection between early conceptions of ecopoetics and the goals of contemporary writers. Namely, the book reveals that while early ecopoetic ideas assume that the world can be viewed objectively and thus represented mimetically, more recent conceptions of the field assume that the world is always experienced subjectively and embraces that subjectivity. In Iijima's collection, several contributors examine antimimetic forms and unnatural environments.

18. Similarly, in "'Sprung from American Soil': The 'Nature' of Africa in the Poetry of Helene Johnson," Katherine Lynes insists on the field's acknowledgment of human life along with nature when she observes that "ecocritical definitions of ecopoetics usually involve advocacy for nature. I concur with this quite logical aim, but I would also argue that there are times when ecocritics should also consider that the focus of ecopoetics is the advocacy for the human subject" (2009, 525). Although here Lynes calls for ecopoetics to engage with the "human subject" as well as "nature," this move is representative of the larger shift toward acknowledging natural and cultural environments that is taking place not only in ecopoetics but throughout ecocritical studies.

19. Iovino and Oppermann lay out the aims of material ecocriticism when they write, "Whereas the interpreters of the 'linguistic turn' stressed the social constructedness (in other words, the artificiality) of discursive practices connected, for example, to the definition of race, class, gender, etc., the 'new materialists' propose an approach that goes beyond the dichotomy between matter and meaning: discursive practices 'intra-act' and are co-extensive with material processes in the many ways the world 'articulates' itself" (2012, 453–54).

20. Language poets are, as explained by Stephen Fredman in *Poet's Prose: The Crisis in American Verse*, "originally critical, practicing a vigilant self-awareness that calls forth language and subjects it to an examination of its mediatory function" (1990, 136–37). Language poetry views language as a construction and demands that readers work to attain meaning from the text.

21. Language poetry's unique concern for self-awareness along with its particular cognizance of language's limitations is directly translated into conceptions of a new ecopoetics. Such connections are apparent in Marcella Durand's identification of the prominent role of language in ecopoetics. In "The Ecology of Poetry," she claims that "experimental ecological poets are concerned with the links between words and sentences, stanzas, paragraphs, and how these systems link with energy and matter—that is, the exterior world" (Durand 2002, 62).

22. Nature's agency is a direct result of theories of material ecocriticism. In *Material Ecocriticism*, Serenella Iovino and Serpil Oppermann contend that "seeking to provide a more accurate (and also more ontologically generous) picture of reality, the new materialists argue for a 'theory of distributive agency,'" through which actions in the world are not caused by "a human subject—posited in isolation from the nonhuman—but a material-semiotic network of human and nonhuman agents incessantly generating the world's embodiments and events" (2014, 3).

23. The chapters work chronologically from Ammons's "Corsons Inlet" (1965), rather than *Garbage* (1993), which was actually published after the first publication of Hejinian's *My Life* in 1987. However, Hejinian's book was released several times, leaving some flexibility in dating it. Since Ammons is often associated with mid-twentieth-century poetics rather than the language poetry movement of the late 1960s and early 1970s with which Hejinian is often associated, I place his work both conceptually and chronologically earlier than Hejinian's.

24. "Corsons Inlet" is often understood for its mimetic form and content. In John Elder's well-known essay on the poem, he observes that the text's formal structure is intended to mimic the ebbs and flows of the shoreline on the page, both through variable line length and punctuation (1996, 146).

25. My argument here extends previous recognitions of naturalcultural intersections in *Garbage*. In "Wallace Stevens and A. R. Ammons as Men on the Dump," Gyorgyi Voros begins to consider the general role of waste in *Garbage*, arguing that it serves both Stevens and Ammons as an equalizing space where high and low, nature and culture, human and nonhuman intermingle. She argues that "the dump disposes of hierarchy, among other things, even to the extent of including nature's waste along with that of human, cultural waste" (2000, 163). In other words, the poet's selection of the dump conflates the human and the natural worlds. No longer separated by hierarchies, within the trash heap everything is intertwined.

26. However, Howe's poem is typically read, as by Marjorie Perloff, as "an elegy for the poet's mother, the Irish actress and playwright Mary Manning," and as a poem interested in "refracting history and language" (Howe 2003, back cover). Although these readings highlight some important projects of *The Midnight*, they fail to recognize how the poem's integration of history, experimentation with language and radical new forms, and infusion of culture are tied to concepts of ecopoetics that seek to foreground the ways in which lived experience in the physical world is always tied to personal memories, history, mental wandering, and the limitations of the senses.

27. Conceptual poetry appropriates found text to create a new poem and generally is concerned with the concept of its creation rather than the product itself. Goldsmith outlines conceptual poetry in *Uncreative Writing* (2011).

# [ 1 ]

# The Material Speaks in
# A. R. Ammons's *Garbage*

*My predisposition, which I hope shortly to justify,*
*is to prefer confusion to oversimplified clarity, meaninglessness*
*to neat, precise meaning, uselessness to overdirected usefulness.*

—A. R. Ammons, "A Poem Is a Walk"

Ammons's affinity for "confusion" rather than "clarity" in the early stages of his career perfectly sums up a pointed desire in his poetry to irritate the fixed or absolute in search of something more flexible and accordingly more authentic to real-world experience. What is at stake in considering the poet's long and highly productive career, though, is what forms best constitute "meaninglessness" over "neat, precise meaning." By employing fluid forms and outlining seemingly authentic natural encounters, much of the poet's early work might readily be identified as ecopoetry for its mimetic form and overt interest in the natural world. In the last decade, poems like "Corsons Inlet," *Sphere*, and *Garbage* have become prominent in ecopoetic approaches to Ammons precisely because of his marked connection to nature and the textual forms that appear to capture it best. In these readings, however, the changes in the poet's work seem to be drowned out by an ongoing obsession with his openly ecocentric and formally mimetic style. Certainly, these are important elements for Ammons; yet, they are aspects of his work that evolve, revert, and even disappear in the latter portion of his career. In late poems, namely *Garbage* (1993), the poet moves beyond the desire to bypass the nature/culture dichotomy at the heart of his earlier work, granting the physical world agency and positioning humans as egocentric rather than ecocentric and form as self-consciously artificial rather than mimetic.

In terms of ecopoetics, Ammons's development throughout his career presents an opportunity to see the potential of unnatural ecopoetics and its differences from traditional understandings of the term. Although the poet's work is often recognized as ecopoetry, unnatural ecopoetics distinguishes readings of Ammons's late poetry from those of his earlier writing, which is especially important since interpretations of his early work often frame how critics read his later poems. From early poems such as "Corsons Inlet" (1965) and *Tape for the Turn of the Year* (1965) to *Garbage* (1993) and *Glare* (1997), the poet's work is commonly read for its connections to tenets of traditional ecopoetics. However, the seeming suitability of his work to conventional conceptions of ecopoetics and other environmentally oriented readings causes some critics to lose sight of ways in which the poet gestures away from traditional conceptions of nature and begins to represent the complexities of naturecultures.

The shifting content of his later work, though, suggests that Ammons is grasping for a new dialogue between humans and their surroundings. *Garbage* is a book-length poem that depicts a Florida trash heap off I-95.[1] Written entirely in unrhymed couplets, the book presents the environment of waste with the same fluid form that characterizes Ammons's earlier work, which often examines more traditionally natural spaces, such as the shoreline in "Corsons Inlet" or the image of the planet in *Sphere*. In its shift away from traditional conceptions of nature, *Garbage* exaggerates an interest in culture that is less prominent in earlier books. In acknowledging the concept of naturecultures in this late poem, I build on efforts by Gyorgyi Voros to establish the significance of the trash heap as a site for nature and culture to fuse. Voros considers Ammons in relation to Wallace Stevens as she investigates the general role of waste for both poets; in *Garbage*, she argues that it serves Ammons as an equalizing space where high and low, nature and culture, human and nonhuman intermingle.[2] She writes: "the dump disposes of hierarchy, among other things, even to the extent of including nature's waste along with that of human, cultural waste" (Voros 2000, 163). In other words, as a result of the unique diversity in the contents of the heap, the poet's selection of the dump conflates the human and the natural worlds. No longer separated by hierarchies, everything is intertwined within the trash heap. Voros's reading of the text marks an important step for Ammons scholarship, as the poet's work begins to gain recognition not only for its mimetic qualities but also for its interest in fusing physical environmental phenomena with the by-products of culture and the limitations of human experience. However, even this compelling approach to *Garbage* minimizes the power that the poet grants to material reality in the text. The book recognizes objects as things and gives them power to act on the page. In doing so, Ammons establishes that while language cannot capture the kind of ecocentrism that he strives for in his earlier work, it can grant things—human and nonhuman, cultural and natural—opportunities to express themselves on the page. In this sense, *Garbage* gives things that are seen as voiceless and powerless, leaving them to go unnoticed in everyday life, the power of expression. In its acknowledgment that humans can never overcome the restrictions of human logic and limitations of language, the book presents a perspective that strives for ecocentrism but also remains self-aware of its inability to ever achieve it.

The garbage heap appears to be the perfect site for naturecultures because it is perceived as a place where the by-products of culture are disposed and decomposed by and into the natural world. Yet, the naturalcultural aspects of the trash heap do not emerge solely from the placement of organic and inorganic elements together, but from the unnatural thing that they become together. The naturalcultural form results from the changes that occur to the contents of the trash heap, leaving the debris of nature and culture altered by one another but not fully decomposed. While the trash heap begins with human and organic material separately, as a result of their processing through the dump, they are neither natural nor cultural but something entirely new and ultimately unnatural. Through the lens of unnatural ecopoetics—a critical mode of reading that considers how the material and nonmaterial elements of environmentality, including physical elements as well as the subjective and cultural peripheral data that bombard the perceiver, are represented in text—a poet who is typically recognized for his mimetic expression of environments through language and form can be acknowledged for the complex interrelations he navigates between nature, culture, and language.

## TRADITIONAL APPROACHES TO AMMONS

Reading *Garbage* through the lens of unnatural ecopoetics bridges the gap between traditional ecopoetic readings of Ammons's poetry and mainstream literary scholarship on his work. Aside from ecopoetic approaches to his poetry, some of the most prominent literary scholars of the twentieth and twenty-first centuries have taken a particular interest in Ammons, presenting arguments that run parallel to the claims I make in this chapter. In fact, scholars such as Bonnie Costello, Harold Bloom, Marjorie Perloff, and Daniel Tobin identify Ammons as everything from a landscape poet to a poet of the Romantic sublime. For instance, in an argument representative of many ecocritical approaches to the poet's work, Daniel Tobin argues that Ammons's approach to nature is comparable to Coleridge's in its attempt to preserve nature's forms and systems in text (1999, 119). For Tobin, as for many other Ammons scholars, the poet's work emerges organically from the natural world. Unnatural ecopoetics calls into question these naturalistic approaches to the poet's work by compelling readers to consider the complex anxieties the poet expresses in *Garbage*—through themes of aging, waning poetic progress, and the pressure for the epic poem—over failures of poetry and language to achieve what earlier poems seemed to optimistically pursue.

While an unnatural ecopoetic reading ultimately recognizes the agential power that Ammons grants the material world in *Garbage*, such a reading initially approaches the poem by building on Bloom's perception of Ammons as employing nature for unnatural purposes. Bloom, one of Ammons's best known and most admiring friends and critics, attempts to distance the poet from nature and instead reads his poetry in the tradition of the Romantic sublime. While many critics, namely Geoffrey Hartman, who is well known for interpreting Ammons's work as overtaken by the voice of nature, argue that nature is the poet's central image, in "A. R. Ammons: The Breaking of the Vessels," Bloom contends that such readings oversimplify how images of nature function in the texts. For example, he writes:

> I myself would say that both Hartman and Ammons are strong misreaders of Ammons, for at least from *Saliences* on he does not write nature-poetry, and indeed I would go back to origins and say truly that he never did write nature-poetry. What Ammons calls "nature," whether he celebrates it or says goodbye to it, is no more natural than Emerson's Nature was, or Whitman's either.... His image, as he admits, is of desire or the will-to-power, what he calls *longing*, and such an image can never be fulfilled by or in nature. (Bloom 1975, 193–94; emphasis in original)

Arguing that Ammons does not write nature poetry but instead engages in a "longing" for transcendence, Bloom contends that nature in Ammons's work is always a point of struggle, as it remains beyond his reach.[3] By identifying nature as a site of longing rather than for mimesis, Bloom illustrates that nature is something with which the poet wrestles but cannot overtake.

Despite the disagreement among scholars about the role of nature in his poetry, Ammons's work lends itself to traditional ecopoetic readings that focus explicitly on the physical environment. These readings of nature in his work are so compelling, in fact, that traditional ecopoetic approaches to the early poetry often reappear in analyses of his late work, despite the many differences in poetic style and social realities between the periods of Ammons's early and late poems. John Elder's 1985 book, *Imagining the Earth: Poetry and the Vision of Nature*, one of the earliest and most prominent examples of ecopoetic theory in action, illustrates how well Ammons's writing lends itself to traditional conceptions of ecopoetics and perhaps why such readings persist across the poet's oeuvre. Elder exemplifies how readings of Ammons's earlier work shape analysis of his later poems in his brief analysis of *Sphere* (1973), a book-length poem that takes the "sphere" of earth as its subject. He writes that "the one long sentence that is Sphere curves out to encompass the birch and shale of landscape closely observed, curves back to join the circle of imagination's 'new coherences'; Ammons's interwoven lines express his 'integral' vision of mind and earth" (Elder 1996, 136). Elder's brief analysis of the poem demonstrates the central characteristics of traditional ecopoetic critique. *Sphere* is read through this lens for its formal attempt to mimic the natural elements of its subject. The "one long sentence" that Elder identifies allows the poet to engage with the vast complexity and interconnections across the globe, a trait that runs through much of his writing and which inspires ecopoetic attention.

Ammons's 1965 poem "Corsons Inlet" possesses traits similar to those identified in Elder's analysis of *Sphere*; specifically, the poem abandons human order and embraces how the disorder of nature shapes the poetic form. The poet conflates the poetic world with the natural realm as the text appears to be shaped not only by human forces but organic ones. Traditional ecopoetic readings by Elder, Scigaj, and Schneider, among others,[4] posit that in the poem language begins to escape limiting forms that impose meanings and becomes closer to expressing an authentic experience in nature. Reading "Corson's Inlet" as an attempt to escape limiting fixed forms seems appropriate given the poem's opening lines. As the speaker begins to embark on a "walk," he moves "to the sea, / then [turns] right along / the surf" (Ammons 1965, 5). The speaker begins by abiding by human forms and ideas of order when he embraces "perpendicular" angles and fixed directions in turning "right" at the sea. The "right" turn, a direction not dictated by natural order but by imposed cultural forces, is directly contrasted by the speaker's subsequent walk. Once he reaches the sea, a site of natural rather than social order, the speaker begins his journey away from rigid human structures and their imposition on nature:

> the walk liberating, I was released from forms,
>     from the perpendiculars,
>         straight lines, blocks, boxes, binds
>     of thought
>     into the hues, shadings, rises flowing bends and blends
>             of sight
>
>                                     (Ammons 1965, 5)

Traditional ecopoetic readings might contend that the walk is, in true Thoreauvian fashion, a "liberating" force because it releases the speaker from anthropocentric ideas of order ("straight lines, blocks, boxes, [and] binds of thought") that restrict his "thought." Later in the poem, the speaker points out that "in nature there are few sharp lines" (6). As such, these forms from which he is liberated are inorganic, occurring in human consciousness as a source of order and containment. These are the "perpendicular" forms that prompt him to turn "right" rather than follow the natural curve of the shoreline. In this sense, these forms impose human order onto nature and make it impossible to experience it authentically or in a pure, unadulterated state. As the speaker moves through the environment and the walk begins to alter his perceptions of nature, these rigid forms are replaced by more fluid and vague concepts ("hues, shadings, rises, flowing bends and blends / of sight"). The speaker moves "into" the flexible and temporal forms that rise, flow, and bend in order to adapt to nature, rather than forcing nature to adapt to a fixed form.

The role of language in translating natural forms to the page is of primary interest to traditional ecopoetic scholars, not only in "Corsons Inlet" but also in readings of much of Ammons's other work. As the speaker of "Corsons Inlet" realizes that the shoreline does not demand logic and order and concedes to the whims of sand, wind, and water, he begins to search for a language with the same flexibility and authenticity to the moment. Elder contends that the fluidity the poet seeks is embodied in the poem through his use of "single unbroken sentences, with colons serving to mark the breaths and to link the poetic elements of variable length" (1996, 146). The colons allow the words on the page to embody a flowing river; the sentences do not reach a syntactic end but simply drift into the next point. As Elder observes, the flowing form of the lines and the syntactic continuity produced by the colons allow the poet to literally erect "no boundaries" and simultaneously to mimic on the page the flows of the shore (Ammons 1965, 6). A traditional ecopoetic reading posits that as the speaker's words begin to move as a force in nature, "inside" and "outside," nature and language, become conflated in the poem.

As a quick look at the opening lines demonstrates, "Corsons Inlet" is well suited to a traditional ecopoetic reading. Its formal elements and ecocentric frame position it well for such critique. The question, though, is whether the same holds true for Ammons's later work. Critics have certainly applied the same traditional ecopoetic principles to *Garbage* and other late poems with great enthusiasm. These arguments are worth consideration for their recognition of Ammons's continued engagement with the natural world and for their insistence on recognizing formal structures as foundational to his poetics. Many traditional ecopoetic readings of the poet's later work, though, resemble the types of readings done of his earlier work, despite the nearly thirty-year gap between his early and late poems. While such readings are productive approaches to *Garbage*, it is worth considering new directions for ecocritical inquiry.

Helen Vendler, Gyorgyi Voros, Leonard Scigaj, Willard Spiegelman, and Frederick Buell identify *Garbage* as reconstituting many of the themes in the poet's early work. Vendler, Spiegelman, and Scigaj, for instance, contend that Garbage exemplifies interconnectedness with the earth by formally mimicking the garbage heap. In "*The Snow Poems* and *Garbage*: Episodes in an Evolving Poetics," Vendler observes: "Since the whole of *Garbage* is a hymn to the necessary principle of extinction (as life is 'consumed with that which it was nourished by,' the enlivening and extinguishing flame of the *calor vitae*), it is of the essence that the poem be engaged in constant change of both genre and diction" (1999, 46; emphasis in original). She argues that the book's shifts in "genre and diction," apparent in the splicing that occurs in the poem along with the speaker's constantly changing tone, are expressive of the poem's external environment as it mimics the variety of objects disposed of in the heap. Scigaj similarly argues, although more explicitly, that nature is the model for the book (1999, 110); and in "Building Up and Breaking Down: The Poetics of Composting," Spiegelman contends that "as a romantic poem organized, at least in part, along the lines of Coleridgean organicism it tries to imitate as well as describe the reality of which it constitutes a part" (1999, 56). These arguments are not unfounded and are certainly worth consideration for how they connect formal structures and experience; however, they attribute Ammons's form and diction to mimesis and do not fully address how the poem's rigid couplet structure or imposed section breaks might problematize interpretations of the structure as mimetic. Similar to alternate interpretations of the text offered by such scholars as Buell and Voros, these analyses of *Garbage* are eerily similar to readings of Ammons's earlier work, namely the most popular for ecopoetic attention, "Corsons Inlet."

Also in the vein of "Corsons" criticism, Buell, Voros, and Scigaj argue that the book demonstrates ecocentrism or biocentrism in its distribution of equality among all natural things—human and nonhuman alike. In "Ammons's Peripheral Vision: *Tape for the Turn of the Year* and *Garbage*," Buell contends that "*Garbage* is not just a high, late point in a major American poet's career, but also a significant opening for the future. *Garbage* is this for a number of different reasons: because it takes the nature tradition past the pastoral and into a thoroughly penetrated, postmodern world; because it faces the limits that even 'postmodern' environmentalism places upon conceptions of nature and faces up to post-humanism as possibly the completest ecocentrism" (1999, 236–37). Buell's analysis posits that in embracing the decay of the trash heap, the book

deals with the inevitable realities of a posthuman world and embraces ecocentrism. In her analysis of Ammons's and Stevens's relationship with trash,
Voros similarly observes that *Garbage* engages with all creatures equally and
foregrounds that equality even from its dedication to those "low on the food
chain" (2000, 167). Like many of Ammons's previous texts, then, *Garbage* is
recognized for its ability to create a level field for all creatures, both through
form and content, thus engaging in what Scigaj identifies as a biocentric poetics
(1999, 85). The prevalence of such themes in the book is undeniable, but the
dominant readings of the text are remarkably similar to readings of the poet's
work from nearly thirty years earlier and, as in ecopoetic readings of the book's
form, seem to overlook the dominance of anthropocentric metapoetic commentary, culturally imposed formal structures, and authorial observation that
permeate and arguably even dominate the book.

Traditional ecopoetic readings posit that *Garbage* attempts to present a
natural poem that is imbued with the physicality of the world through its ecocentrism, metapoetic commentary on recycled language, and mimetic form.
As with "Corsons," scholars observe that *Garbage* takes on a form that mimics
its environment, arguing, as Scigaj does, that not only is the physical environment the impetus for the poem but the trash heap shapes its form (1999, 110).
Similarly, Vendler attributes the book's form to the physical environment when
she identifies its mimetic quality, which she views as an impetus to real-world
activism from the reader.[5] While these conventional ecopoetic approaches
to *Garbage* are commonplace, they do not encapsulate the breadth of recent
Ammons scholarship. Costello, for instance, argues that Ammons is using the
natural elements of the text to fuel his "rhetorical vision" and that the rhetorical takes precedence in the poem. She contends that the poet is

> offering the soil as the object and model of man's intelligence. Ammons
> often hovers around an immanentist mode which abandons all rheto-
> ricity in the presence of the particular, but his imagination never truly
> entertains the primitive. While he enjoys those moments when poetic
> authority is disarmed by natural presence, the submissive or natural
> voice is often a foil for a highly rhetorical vision. (Costello 1989, 420).

In this sense, she argues that the soil is not a model but a tool that the poet uses
strategically and not blindly. Thus, the argument so prominent in traditional
ecopoetic readings that the poem embodies the natural world, speaking for it
through form and metapoetic commentary, is troubled by critics like Costello.
Andrew Zawacki similarly challenges the primacy of nature in Ammons's work
in "Ego and Eco: Saying 'I' in *Expressions of Sea Level*." Here, Zawacki reminds

readers of the simple fact that "the poem and the book have inevitably been said by the human. That is, the poet can't get out of the way: any attempts to write *by* sea level are destined to be haunted by the insistence of what is being said *about* sea level.... Eco is constantly remanded to the ego" (2012, 51). Despite the widespread readings to the contrary, especially within ecocriticism, poetry scholars have begun to recognize that even though Ammons's poetics is tied to the natural world, he cannot replace his own self or "ego" with the "eco." The human is always the intermediary between the two worlds.

Evidently, Ammons's work aligns well with traditional theories of eco-poetics, which are primarily interested in poetic mimicry of natural environments. The poet's interest in language and form coupled with his prolonged fascination with nature lends itself to ecopoetic analysis. Yet, as Gyorgyi Voros points out, Ammons's "mirroring" of the natural world fails. In "Earth's Echo: Answering Nature in Ammons's Poetry," Voros observes: "Vision in Ammons...expressed in tropes of looking, seeing, and mirroring, is most often the mechanism for failed negotiations of the incongruence between human and nonhuman worlds" (2002, 93). Voros recognizes that despite all of his efforts throughout his poetics, Ammons's work never achieves congruency with nature but always remains one step removed. The doubt that surrounds Ammons's ecopoetics becomes more identifiable in his later poetry, such as *Garbage*, where the exalted power of nature becomes troubled. Yet, most eco-poetic scholars do not readily embrace the depth of this failure or consider how it fundamentally alters the foundation of the poet's work. As a result, Ammons's late poems are read in much the same way as his early work, for their ecocentric, mimetic, and natural elements.

## AN UNNATURAL ECOPOETIC READING OF *GARBAGE*

Unnatural ecopoetics presents new possibilities for reading Ammons's work by identifying the dominant presence of naturecultures in *Garbage* and, even more importantly, locating the textual space where those naturalcultural elements are exposed and made active. The case for a traditional ecopoetic reading of *Garbage* is strong and certainly has its merits. However, such readings appear to be predicated on understandings of Ammons's earlier poems and are infused with critical interpretations of his earlier work. Looking backward in the poet's career may be useful in understanding the text, but it is important to remember that *Garbage* is in many ways quite different from the poet's previous writing and might be expressing different sentiments. With that in mind, I take a new approach to *Garbage* through the lens of unnatural ecopoetics in which the book's form, naturalcultural elements, metapoetic commentary, and ecocentrism, which make it so ripe for traditional ecopoetic readings, are viewed from a new perspective. Through this new lens, *Garbage* attains a new relevance in ecopoetic studies.

The trash heap is considered by many critics of Ammons's book to be a sort of peripherally natural space, where nature recycles the waste of human civilization back to the earth. Scholars often view Ammons's trash heap as cleansing, a reading that mirrors broader attitudes toward waste, such as Susan Signe Morrison's, which contend that waste and dirt have restorative abilities "to *charge*, catalyzing ethical behavior and profound insights, even compassion" (2015, 3). Voros similarly argues that "rubbish is material approaching a condition analogous to that of wilderness in nature" and that the theme of *Garbage* is the "possibility for resacrilizing trash as the necessary prelude to rebirth and regeneration" (2000, 173–74). Likening garbage to the natural environment and promoting its regenerative role, Voros and others view the theme of the book as garbage and its promising power to regenerate the world. The book's speaker, though, not only presents garbage itself as regenerative for the world but proposes that the trash heap is a space of new creations, where natural-cultural fusions do not bring complete decay or complete creation, but something in between—something new. Practically speaking, as one Department of Health and Environmental Control confirms, trash does not completely break down nor decompose when placed in a landfill ("Landfills" 2013, 2). However, it does begin the process, changing from its original state but not promising rebirth for hundreds or even thousands of years. Instead of a recycling or transformation, the book's literal setting on the trash heap provides a metaphorical space where material and nonmaterial elements that shape experiences in the world become evident and active. In the trash heap, human and nonhuman material elements begin to act as they alter and shape language in new ways. Trash is not a symbol of promise and rejuvenation for the earth nor of decay and destruction that necessarily constitutes the kind of call to political action that traditional ecopoetic readings posit. Ammons's garbage is a site of natural-cultural fusions, but those elements of the text are made apparent and active only through the poem's textual space.

Unnatural ecopoetics recognizes both the role of nature in the garbage dump and the alterations that occur as it fuses with cultural debris, ultimately revealing that language does not enter the trash heap and emerge entirely new, clean, and purified, as a traditional ecopoetic reading might posit, but as a version of itself, covered with the detritus of decay, filth, and dirt. Garbage, the symbol of culture throughout the book, does change in the trash heap but it reemerges with a naturalcultural tint, still itself but changed by natural processes and imbued with the filth of its own decay along with the natural elements that facilitate it. As such, the speaker states that "life is like a poem: the moment it / begins, it begins to end" (Ammons 1993, 66). Mingling language with "life," the speaker reveals that its relevance hinges on novelty and newness.

Unnatural ecopoetics engages with the remnants of culture that are altered by the filth of decay that stays with it and revels in the new naturalcultural object that is created within the textual space of the poem. This occurs in the poem, first, as the speaker foregrounds the poet's influence on the scene through self-reflexive commentary and imposed formal structures; second, by acknowledging how, like the literal garbage in the poem that retains some of its self but is simultaneously altered by the dump, the remnants of words' former meanings and usages—remnants like external connotations, former contexts, or similar words—interfere with any mimetic approach to representation; and third, by considering how the filth of natural decay that coats the objects in the trash heap facilitates a more accurate textual rendering of the complexity, imperfection, and confusion that surrounds real-world experience.

First, unnatural ecopoetics reveals that in *Garbage* the textual space is created through self-reflexive commentary on the poet's life and influence on the page as well as through fixed formal structures. Interestingly, the book is considered by some critics to have a mimetic form;[6] yet, it could be considered one of Ammons's more artificial forms. Like *Glare*, another of the poet's long poems, *Garbage* is written almost exclusively in unrhymed couplets and in the poet's signature style flows smoothly through fluid colons, entirely without end stops. While the colons in "Corsons Inlet" certainly have a fluidity, in *Garbage* they often act more as end points or radical departures. The colons signal jumps, for instance, from moments of deep personal reflection on the role of the poet, to the meanings of words, to a material location, not to demonstrate disjuncture alone but to highlight the new meaning that is created through their connection: I'm a

> hole puncher or hole plugger: stick a finger
> in the dame (*dam*, damn, dike), hold back the issue
>
> of creativity's flood, the forthcoming, futuristic,
> the origins feeding trash: down by I-95 in
>
> Florida where flatland's ocean- and gulf-flat,
> mounds of disposal rise

(1993, 18)

Here, the colon cannot be seen only for its fluidity, as traditional ecopoetic readings often posit, but for its presentation of disjunctive elements. When the speaker's reflection on his role as poet ("hole plugger") fuses not only with commentary on words, pronunciations, and divergent meanings ("dame (*dam*, damn, dike)") but also with the material location of the trash heap ("down by I-95 in // Florida"), the colon serves as a point of departure. Rather than brushing the departure aside, an unnatural ecopoetic lens focuses on the colon's ability to distinguish the poet's subjectivity by placing his emotional involvement, mental wandering, and physical location side by side. Together, the divergent elements create a truly disjunctive scene—one in which real-world experience is not presented as unrealistically composed but rather disconnected, random, and yet somehow still meaningful. Put another way, the colons need not mimic the physical environment of the trash heap in order to convey the poet's experience because the real-world encounter from which the poet writes is, like the poem, a tangled web of subjective thoughts, sights, and anxieties.

The colons in *Garbage* mark a moment of connection between dissimilar things and often serve to combine the material world with the nonmaterial reflection of the speaker. The poem's use of colons along with its rigid conformity to the unrhymed couplet suggest that *Garbage* is not mimetic in its form but, rather, rigidly fixed—a formal choice that in no way mirrors the indiscriminate chaos of the real-world trash heap it is often said to mimic. In fact, an unnatural ecopoetic reading recognizes the poem as actively working to expose the influence of the poet through a highly emphasized formal structure that reiterates his presence throughout.

While traditional readings of the book overlook its naturalcultural dimension, unnatural ecopoetics reveals that *Garbage* is uniquely self-aware of the poet's influence and consistently dedicated to preserving the innate power of the material world on the page. The self-reflexive form of the book is reiterated through the voice of the aging poet, and the agency of the material world is distinctly expressed in his reflections on his own life. As the speaker debates whether he is going to "write that great poem / the world's waiting for," he emphasizes the authorial intrusion on lived experience (13). Although the poem responds to the literal space of a landfill "down by I-95 in // Florida," the speaker reminds the reader throughout the book that the poet's voice acts as an intermediary or frame for the experience. Such self-reflexivity is coupled with the poem's consideration of the power of the material world. The speaker states that "trees defined themselves (into // various definitions) through a dynamics of / struggle" (15). By employing an action verb, the speaker immediately grants the trees agential power. The lines that follow document the importance of "dense competition" among trees in order to keep them healthy (15). In this way, the speaker grants the material world a sense of action and meaning that is often reserved only for the human actor. Once the material attains agency, it becomes clear that the speaker employs the actions of the trees in order to comment on the inability of humans to exercise self-control in their own lives. In a clear response to the gluttonous waste of the trash heap, the speaker imparts his naturalcultural sentiments to the reader, stating "we tie into the / lives of those we love and our lives, then, go // as theirs go; their pain we can't shake off (16–17). The speaker's sentiments clearly create a world where natural and cultural elements are both active.

A second way in which the poem engages with an unnatural ecopoetic reading of naturecultures is through language. When language fails in the poem, it highlights the limited ability of words to accurately express lived experience.[7] In *Garbage*, Ammons demonstrates that when language attempts to express raw reality, it is destined to fail. Harkening back to William Carlos Williams's charge to "make it new," Ammons presents novelty as a way around the barrier between nature and culture, as he argues that making language new can make it more accurate to the world. However, the task of novelty is not an easy one for Ammons's speaker. As he struggles with the balance of nature and culture in the effort to write a poem instilled with such novelty, he overtly contemplates naturalcultural elements of the trash heap and the persistent limitations of language.

> but we are natural: nature, not
>
> we, gave rise to us: we are not, though, though
> natural, divorced from higher, finer configurations:
>
> tissues and holograms of energy circulate in
> us and seek and find representations of themselves
>
> outside us, so that we can participate in
> celebrations high and know reaches of feeling
>
> and sight and thought that penetrate (really
> penetrate) far, far beyond these our wet cells,
>
> right on up past our stories, the planets, moons,
> and other bodies locally to the other end of
>
> the pole where matter's forms diffuse and
> energy loses all means to express itself except
>
> as spirit

> (21)

Only a few lines after commenting on "dead language" and its reemergence from the dump, the speaker here considers the possibilities of naturalcultural unions and the challenges that remain for language despite the landfill's reconstitution of it. He establishes the inherent interrelation of nature and culture when he comments that "nature, not // we, gave rise to us," implying the natural roots of humanity, but quickly reminds the reader that humans are also infused with the "finer configurations" of culture. Both natural and cultural, humans maintain a capacity to reach "outside" themselves in order to comprehend the "feeling // and sight and thought that penetrate" beyond the limitations of the human body ("far beyond these our wet cells"). Through this "higher" thinking that we might consider to be culture, the speaker explains that humans can move "past our stories" and even beyond knowledge ("the planets, moons, / and other bodies locally") to places where "matter's forms diffuse and / energy loses all means to express itself," leaving only inexpressibility and thus incomprehensibility. In these formless places facilitated by human culture, matter can express itself only "as spirit," a vague and intangible expression. In this spirit, the "mind" is identified as the only thing that "abides, the eternal," a force that is both "momentary" and long-lasting ("having // been there so long") because while the eternal cannot sustain a single form and is constantly changing ("turns into another pear or sunfish"), it has sustained power over the mind that allows it to remain ever-present.

> there, oh, yes, in the abiding where
> mind but nothing else abides, the eternal,
>
> until it turns into another pear or sunfish,
> that momentary glint in the fisheye having
>
> been there so long, coming and going, it's
> eternity's glint: it all wraps back round,
>
> into and out of form, palpable and impalpable,
> and in one phase, the one of grief and love,
>
> we know the other, where everlastingness comes to
> sway, okay and smooth: the heaven we mostly
>
> want, though, is this jet-hoveled hell back,
> heaven's daunting asshole: one must write and
>
> rewrite till one writes it right
>
> (21–22)

The speaker goes on to reveal that the eternal shifts "into and out of form," sometimes becoming "palpable" and sometimes "impalpable." The human can truly "know" the eternal or "everlastingness" only as an emotion or feeling ("grief and love") and not through the mind, which is grasping constantly at a fixed "hovel" or structure that is "daunting" the perceiver toward failure with the promise of stability.

Although this passage seems to be disconnected from the image of both garbage and language, it appears just after the book's most pronounced connection between the two, when the speaker proclaims that "there is a mound, // too, in the poet's mind dead language is hauled / off to" (20), and in the few subsequent lines between his discussion of "dead language" and naturecultures, the speaker asks "where // but in the grief of failure, loss, error do we / discern the savage afflictions that turn us around" (21). The failure that precedes the poet's discussion of naturecultures informs the conclusion of the passage that writing is endlessly destined to fail. In his acknowledgment that humans always seek ways of knowing and understanding that allow fixity rather than feeling, the speaker reveals that the demand for concrete knowledge and comprehension brings with it a failure of language. He claims that "one must write and // rewrite till one writes it right," realizing that to "write it right" is always impossible since language is multiplicitous and always moving as "everlastingness comes to / sway, okay, and smooth." The mind's demand for such knowing and the quest for writing to express it lead to an inevitable failure of language that permeates the book. As such, immediately following this circular failure, the speaker embarks on a rant in which he questions his own relevance (22).

The relevance of the poet's work largely hinges on his view of language and the fluidity that he identifies throughout the book. In his 1993 essay "On *Garbage*," Ammons comments on how the call to "write it right" correlates with his poetics. He claims, "I have since the sixties . . . tried to get some kind of rightness into improvisations. The arrogance implied by getting something right the first time is incredible, but no matter how much an ice-skater practices, when she hits the ice it's all a one-time event" (1996, 125). Here, the speaker's claim that to "write it right" is problematic corresponds to how the poet explores language in *Garbage*. Later in the book, it becomes clear that language cannot escape its "meaning" or connotations no matter how much it is recreated, recycled, or cleansed in the dump:

> meaninglessness is the

> providence, the wiping clear of planes where we
> can structure possibility into whatever housings

level out: the antecedent of meaning is not
meaning always, meaning which could direct,

delimit, interfere, but the absence of meaning:
we should be pretty happy with the possibilities

and limits we can play through emergences free
of complexes of Big Meaning, but is there

really any meaninglessness
. . . . . . . . . . . . . . . . . . . .

there is truly *only* meaning,
only meaning, meanings, so many meanings,

meaninglessness becomes what to make of so many
meanings

                                    (85–86; emphasis in original)

The initial praise for "meaninglessness" in this passage is related to the speaker's
desire to "write it right" or make it authentic. Only when language is free of
"meaning which could direct, // delimit, interfere," a discussion that appears to
mirror the earlier consideration of fixity as opposed to flexibility, can it remain
fresh and free to express the reality of the moment. Meaning, the ultimate goal
of language, restricts "possibilities." Despite the pitfalls of meaning, the speaker
concludes that "there is *only* meaning" and "so many meanings," in fact, that
they bring a sense of "meaninglessness." In other words, when words can mean
many things at once, the result is no meaning at all.

Recognizing multiple meanings in this passage, the speaker engages in a
self-reflective consideration of language that both connects to the central garbage image and explains his own self-proclaimed poetic failure. Reiterating
how the garbage metaphor relates to language, the discussion of meaning here
is particularly relevant to a broader discussion of how language reemerges
from the landfill. While a traditional ecopoetic reading might argue that words
emerge purified, when this passage is read through an unnatural ecopoetic
lens, it can be seen as saying that regardless of change or cleansing, language
continues to point to meanings because it is always infused with its multiple
usages and contexts. In this passage, then, it becomes clear that the union of
nature and culture within the landfill does not allow words to be new, and this
outcome prompts the speaker to acknowledge his own inevitable failure. The
impending failure of language that concludes section two of the book begins
when the speaker comments on the contribution of culture to humanity. When

he engages purely with the mind, he reaches an impasse, unable to "write it right." The speaker uncovers the inability of language to accurately express the impossible "eternal" that the mind seeks when he begins again in section three by accepting the limitations of language and thus the poem, limitations that are reiterated throughout the remainder of the book.

When he accepts the confines of his writing, the speaker announces, "I have to start // again from a realization of failure" (56). In this metapoetic moment, the speaker comments on the inevitable failure of the poem. Beginning with the "realization of failure," he foregrounds the inability of the poem to ever truly express the reality behind it. Despite the failure, though, he is compelled to write, claiming that his

> rhetoric goes on, though, with a terrible
>
> machine-like insistence whether potholes
> appear in the streets or not, or knots in my
>
> line, or furriers in my traps
>
> (57)

Referring to his writing as "rhetoric" and describing it as having a "machine-like insistence," the speaker explains that despite its inability to express accurately, writing persists. He concedes that his writing is filled with "potholes," "knots," and "furriers" that complicate meaning, but despite those divergences, the poet insists and his writing meanders toward meaning. Foregrounding language's limitations in this way is central to unnatural ecopoetics. In recognizing these boundaries, poetry approaches poetic expressions of the world tentatively and fully cognizant and forthcoming about its own limitations. The foregrounding of poetic limits is unique to unnatural ecopoetics because traditional understandings of the field imply parity between the physical world and its expression in language. By accepting and highlighting language's limitations, though, unnatural ecopoetic readings consider more accurately the multiple elements, including the author's own subjective perspective and style, that compose a literary expression of real-world experience.

An unnatural ecopoetic reading of *Garbage* thus contends that the failure of language articulated throughout the book brings with it the acknowledgement that words, while not pure, remain significant. This reading ties directly to the book's central image of trash and its relation to how words function and change. Beyond the recognition of the limitations of language, the third major argument of such a reading is that words emerge from the landfill altered by the grime of natural degeneration, but are more accurate referents to the world when dipped in the naturalcultural filth of the trash heap. In one of the book's late puzzling moments, the speaker appears to comment on the enhanced possibility of language that is tied to both the physical and human worlds:

the other side of anything is worth

nearly as much as the side: the difference
so slight in fact, that one goes out to see if

it is there: I want a curvature like the
arising of a spherical section, a sweep that

doesn't break down from arc into word, image,
definition, story, thesis, but all these

assimilated to an arch of silence, an interrelation
permitting motion in stillness: I want to see

furrows of definition, both the centerings of
furrow and the clumpy outcastings beyond: I do

not want to be caught inside for clarity: I
want clarity to be a smooth long bend

disallowing no complexity in coming clean

(92–93)

Here, the speaker begins by acknowledging the multiple meanings or sides of all things ("the other side of anything is worth // nearly as much as the side") and explains that the promise of multiple meanings inspires individuals to take action ("one goes out to see if // it is there"). Immediately connecting idea to action, this passage ties the discussion to language, a connection that is made more explicit when he explains that he wants "a curvature" "that doesn't break down from arc into word, image, / definition, story, thesis." In calling for an "arc," a physical shape, that cannot be broken down into its parts, namely its narrative roles, but instead remains one complete whole, the speaker seeks something that fuses the physical with language. The fusion that he seeks would create something physical and composed in part of language, but still silent ("all these // assimilated to an arch of silence, an interrelation / permitting motion in stillness"). The silence that the speaker calls for here is predicated on a movement away from being "caught inside for clarity," a direct connection to the inside/outside or nature/culture dichotomy that permeates this unnatural ecopoetic reading. Claiming that he does not want to be "caught inside" in order to attain clarity and "definition," he declares that what he wants is a clarity that emerges slowly and smoothly from an acceptance of complexity ("I / want clarity to be a smooth long bend // disallowing no complexity in coming clean").

Unnatural ecopoetics prompts readers to consider this passage for its attention to "interrelation" and investigate this union in relation to the book's central image of the landfill. Here, the speaker explains that words are inadequate in themselves because they are "caught inside" a search for "clarity" that hinges on single definitions rather than "furrows of definition" that are composed both of those popular meanings at the center and those unseemly connotations on the periphery ("both the centerings of / furrow and the clumpy outcastings beyond"). As the speaker ties his discussion to language and definition, he calls for a language that is composed of multiple meanings and infused with the physicality of shape ("an arch"). So as the speaker articulates his goals in this passage—his desire for a single channel for both complex language and the physical world—he meanderingly explains the central thrust of the book. *Garbage* is a text that demonstrates not a recycling but, alternatively, a muddying of language that occurs through the metaphor of the landfill. As words enter and reemerge from the trash heap, they are changed into objects infused with the natural and cultural debris that accompanied them through the dump. In this way, a word emerges precisely as what the speaker claims to seek— "a sweep that // doesn't break down from arc into word, image, / definition, story, thesis," and in holding together, it retains "all these // assimilated" into a single force. Language cannot be distinguished as language in and of itself after working through the landfill, and thus one cannot remain "caught inside" the linguistic system, searching "for clarity" from within, but instead must turn outward toward the "complexity" and connectedness of the physical world to make meaning.

## CONCLUSION

Unnatural ecopoetics presents a new approach to poets like Ammons, who have traditionally been read for their connections to the natural world without fully considering how those ties are troubled in the texts. While reading early poems like "Corsons Inlet" as mimetic or attempting to mirror the natural world may help elucidate that piece and even that historical moment, critics must consider how developments in personal, technological, and social spaces might change a writer's poetics over time. For Ammons, early poems like "Corsons Inlet" are only beginning to explore the relationship between the natural world and the human perceiver. Late poems like *Garbage* stem from the poet's own experience and the changes that have unfolded around him. Exposed to a world of rapidly developing and engulfing technology and faced with the anxiety of his own aging, the Ammons of *Garbage* explores the human relationship with the physical world with more complexity and doubt over his ability to succeed than in his earlier texts. Recognizing these developments as a central part of his later work, unnatural ecopoetics reveals that *Garbage* draws out naturecultures by foregrounding the textuality of a literal space where nature and culture intersect.

When Ammons proclaims that "garbage has to be the poem of our time," he explicitly tells the reader that this later text emerges out of a set of physical and cultural realities of waste that are caused largely by technological advances of the late twentieth century (1993, 18). Yet, this aspect of the text is often ignored by traditional ecopoetic readings that emphasize nature over culture and are better suited to the poet's earlier work. Unnatural ecopoetics contends that *Garbage* uses the trash heap as "the poem of our time" because the rise of a commodified technology culture has created a new environment in which the natural world is no longer distinguishable from the cultural space. In this contemporary natureculture, all things are constantly becoming waste as they quickly cycle through the flash of their own relevance. Demonstrating the poet's interest in naturecultures rather than nature or culture in isolation as previous critics have, unnatural ecopoetics opens up a new direction of inquiry in Ammons scholarship, where the cultural is not secondary to the natural but a necessary part of it. Reading *Garbage* in this way reveals that naturalcultural unions are present in a wide variety of texts, including those that are traditionally recognized as examples of ecopoetics for their attention to the natural world.

An unnatural ecopoetic reading of *Garbage* is focused on the poet's creation of a textual space through self-reflexive language and form and his creation of a naturalcultural environment where the material world expresses its agency. In the punctuated textual space of the poem, it becomes clear that Ammons's book is not primarily about garbage itself; the book is ultimately about the metaphorical power of waste in highlighting the unlikely environments where nature and culture interconnect. By identifying garbage as a site of naturalcultural fusion, the book reveals the material and nonmaterial elements that compose the poet's environmental experience. When human and nonhuman materialities combine in the heap, the metaphorical space of the poem demonstrates the agential power of those materials.

NOTES

1. The poet locates the trash heap with the lines "down by 1-95 in // Florida" the "garbage trucks crawl as if in obeisance, / as if up ziggurats toward the high places gulls // and garbage keep alive" (Ammons 1993, 18).

2. The view of garbage as a site for rejuvenation and blending is represented in recent ecocritical scholarship on waste. In "Languages of Waste: Matter and Form in our Garb-age," Véronique Bragard contends that "manufactured waste [is a] substance that threatens but also interconnects" (2013, 462). Susan Signe Morrison similarly argues for the positive power of garbage in *The Literature of Waste: Material Ecopoetics and Ethical Matter* (2015).

3. In his analysis of *Plunder*, Bloom observes that "Nature proclaims the poet's mind as its despoiler, and Ammons, despite his pride, manifests anxiety as to the dictation involved. Yet whatever kind of a poem we want to call this, it is no version of pastoral, for implicitly the poet tells us that nature was never his home" (1975, 198). To some extent, this reading parallels Bonnie Costello's reading, in which she contends that nature serves as a tool for the poet's own revelations. In "The Soil and Man's Intelligence," Costello similarly challenges the central role given nature when she contends that Ammons should be read for the parallels he draws between language and landscape rather than his mimesis. She writes that in Ammons's work "language is not so much part of nature (as in [Gary] Snyder) as nature, or things observed in nature, are like language.... We are reminded repeatedly that this poet is looking at nature not for itself but for what it can offer the imagination" (Costello 1989, 424). Although like Bloom's analysis this reading of Ammons's work is not identified by the critic as an ecopoetic lens, Costello's reading supports a movement toward what I identify as an unnatural ecopoetic reading, in which self-reflexive language and formal experimentation foregrounds a textual space where the material and nonmaterial elements of environmentality are exposed.

4. Elder argues that in "Corsons Inlet" "the emphasis is on the way in which nature and the poet alike break open old orders continually, to liberate the materials from which new orders may be 'grasped.'... Accordingly, the world of Ammons's poetry is always presented as a freshly emerging event" (1996, 144). His desire to create an untainted moment on the page that can convey the novelty of real-world experience is precisely what aligns Ammons's work with much traditional ecopoetic theory. Although more explicitly than Elder, in *Sustainable Poetry: Four American Ecopoets*, Scigaj similarly identifies Ammons's attention to natural order as an attempt to express the prelinguistic moment; he observes that such moves are staples of traditional ecopoetics: "Within ecopoetry and environmental poetry, language is often foregrounded only to reveal its limitations, and this is accomplished in such a way that the reader's gaze is thrust beyond language back into the less limited world that language refers to, the inhabited place where human must live in harmony with ecological cycles" (Scigaj 1999, 38). Scigaj and Elder acknowledge the ways that original experiences are altered as they are translated through poetry and seek to move the "reader's gaze" to the "less limited" world of natural order. Thus, Scigaj and Elder argue that Ammons's ecopoetics in "Corsons Inlet" is an ecocentric one, as it acknowledges the natural world as equal to that of humans.

5. Vendler contends that "the point of all Ammons's unsettling changes (thematic, generic, lexical) is to mimic a universe constituted of continual creations and destructions, to ratify a metaphysics acceding to the necessity of change, and to announce an ethics of protest, urgent (if helplessly so) against the human waste entailed by the universal principles of destruction" (1999, 47). For Vendler, the poem attempts to "mimic" the physical space of the trash heap in an effort to encourage real-world action from the reader that would acknowledge and change

the destructive habits of waste that permeate human culture. Her argument closely aligns with the principles of traditional ecopoetics. In *Ecopoetry: A Critical Introduction*, J. Scott Bryson specifically identifies one of the central characteristics of ecopoetry as a warning of the impending risk lurking in human actions (2002, 5–6). Here, Vendler appears to identify such a trait in Ammons's poem.

6. Scigaj contends that in the book "nature, not language, is the model for the poem's structure" (1999, 110).

7. Scott Knickerbocker's *Ecopoetics: The Language of Nature, the Nature of Language*, which I would identify as a step toward a theory of unnatural ecopoetics, contends that this new version of ecopoetics must embrace its own artifice and even foreground its own limitations to contend with the challenges presented by postmodern theories that problematize mimesis (2012, 2).

# From Perception to Text in
# Lyn Hejinian's *My Life*

*The meaning of a word in its place*
*derives both from the word's lateral reach,*
*its contacts with its neighbors in a statement,*
*and from its reach through and out of the text into the outer world,*
*the matrix of its contemporary and historical reference.*

—LYN HEJINIAN, *Language of Inquiry*

REFLECTING ON HER OWN POETRY, Lyn Hejinian emphasizes that the meaning of words must be determined by their context and continually rejuvenated to match that context.[1] Throughout her poetry, the connections between perception, language, and experience are central to the poet's struggle with how to best express the complexities or, in her terms, multiplicity of experience in the limited form of language.[2] Although this pronounced struggle with perception and language becomes increasingly evident in her later work, it is formative in *My Life* (1980),[3] her most popular and seemingly most personal text. The book, which is presented as autobiographical, reveals that even in the rendering of the most personal moments and events, the poet is pulled in multiple directions at once, always trapped behind the limitations of the words themselves and the boundaries of her own perception. The poet's struggle to express the multiplicity of her own life experiences, including their natural and cultural infusions, in the limited medium of language compels her toward formal experimentation, language play, and self-reflexive commentary that reveals the text's own limitations, making it ripe for an unnatural ecopoetic reading that can specifically acknowledge the foregrounded textual space created by the poet and its exposure of naturalcultural entanglements. Through this lens, it becomes clear that Hejinian creates her autobiography not by telling stories of her past that are only weak copies of the events themselves but by textually recreating the multiplicity of original material experiences and preserving their complex interrelations with the nonmaterial elements of those encounters.

*My Life* is an unlikely environment for an ecopoetic or even ecocritical reading since the poet's work is not heavily invested in traditional environments and makes little reference to natural elements. In fact, her work might be seen as entirely unnatural, both literally in terms of the book's frame as autobiography and figuratively in its exploration of the capacities and limitations of language in capturing real-world experiences. There is some precedent for connecting material experience with text in Hejinian's poetry, and while this previous work does not come to an understanding of the poet's triangulation of language, form, and self-reflection, it begins to consider the complexity of her poetics, which facilitates an unnatural ecopoetic reading. Marjorie Perloff, Megan Simpson, and Charles Altieri, for instance, have considered how Hejinian's inquiries into language work toward a more accurate expression of experience, which propels criticism toward questions about the relationship between the physical world and linguistic expressions of it in her work, questions that are central to the ecopoetic approach taken up here. Megan Simpson begins to work toward the role of subjective experience in the poet's work. In *Poetic Epistemologies: Gender and Knowing in Women's Language-Oriented Writing*, she specifically considers Hejinian's emphasis on experiences of reality over objective representations of it, an emphasis she identifies as vital to her poetics (2000, 12). Identifying the gap between how one perceives and understands their lived experience and the experience itself, Simpson rightly identifies the centrality of the physical encounter in the poet's writing. While Hejinian's work appears primarily concerned with telling the story of her life, it is largely occupied with navigating the disjunction between an original event and conceptions of it.

For the poet, contending with the subjectivity inherent in her perception of lived experience demands a poetics that acknowledges its own limitations. Like Simpson, Charles Altieri views Hejinian's poems as deeply engaged with preserving subjectivity at any cost, regardless of the logical structure or meaning of the poetry produced as a result (1998, 178). Altieri's argument helps explain the poet's disjunctive style while simultaneously revealing the prominence of subjectivity in her poetics. As Marjorie Perloff writes in *Radical Artifice: Writing Poetry in the Age of Media*, the poet's ability to formally adapt real-world encounters to text is through "reluctance" and a "deferral of meaning and denial of plenitude that is central to Hejinian's conception of writing" (1991, 168). Altieri and Perloff show that throughout Hejinian's writing the turn away from fixity and objectivity facilitates the creation of textual spaces that attempt to create the subjective experience of the physical world on the page.

In preserving subjectivity, the poet reveals the power that language holds not only in communicating but also in shaping conceptions of experience. For Hejinian, language is not only a tool but also a force in itself that has the ability to affect how material reality is encountered, perceived, and expressed. Simpson similarly contends that language is both a tool and an agential force in the poet's work when she observes that "Hejinian's many poetic works—open, elliptical, ongoing—demonstrate and explore the epistemological problem of 'the real' that we are faced with when we acknowledge that language plays more than a merely descriptive role in our knowledge of the world" (2000, 12). The power that language attains in Hejinian's poetry is arguably a central aspect of her poetics. As a result of its prominence, in fact, many scholars read the poet for her connection to language writing. David Huntsperger, for instance, positions Hejinian as a language poet who is principally concerned with politics (Huntsperger 2010, 13). Although the poet's political agenda is not particularly relevant to this discussion, Huntsperger shows that her poetry is uniquely rooted in real-world issues. It appears, then, that Hejinian's ability to embrace subjectivity and express the disjunction inherent in lived experience is rooted in her connection to language poetry.

## LANGUAGE POETRY, NEW MATERIALISMS, AND ECOPOETICS

What is perhaps less clear than Hejinian's incontrovertible roots in language writing is the link between language poetry and ecopoetics. While some ecopoetic theorists and scholars might contend that the language writing movement's political connections are similar to the environmental activism at the heart of some traditional ecopoetic theories, the connection between ecopoetics and language writing runs much deeper.[4] While language poetry appears entirely disconnected from the physical world and certainly from traditional ideas of nature, it is deeply invested in analyzing modes of perception and the presence of subjectivity in everyday experience. Linda Reinfeld specifically defines the movement in these terms in *Language Poetry: Writing as Rescue* (1992). She describes language poetry as a movement "both conceptually sophisticated and elegantly made that embodies a sense of language rooted not in some vague sentimental conception of nature but in the specific constructions of thought" (1992, 3). In essence, the movement considers how individuals conceive of experience and ultimately how those experiences are expressed in language.

Similar to Reinfeld's points, Juliana Spahr identifies language writing's interest in disjunction in *Everybody's Autonomy: Collective Reading and Collective Identity* (2001). She contends that

> Western languages support and are supported by the mercantile tendencies of society, which valorize that which can be counted: the grammatical subject/object. The subject of the sentence is always an object—a person, place, or thing—and is given hierarchical priority…. The emphasis on disjunction and the nonstandard grammatical economy that accompanies much language writing challenges the assumption that language is an individual affair, a segregated mode of expressive correspondence that is unconnected to larger social apparatuses. (2001, 56)

For Spahr, language writing's upheaval of narrative standards is directly related to a turn against social norms that impose limitations on language. Through language writing, the poet can liberate him or herself from those limitations and become "unconnected" from those social systems that might inhibit meaning. Spahr's understanding of the field is not radically dissimilar from mainstream definitions of it. For instance, in the first issue of *L=A=N=G=U=A=G=E Magazine* published in 1978, Lawrence Weiner writes, "It (language) seems to be the least impositional means of transferring information concerning the relationships of human beings with materials from one to another (source)" (8). Language poetry, then, is embarking on the "least impositional" method of expressing the complexity of real-world experiences, a sentiment that lies at the core of ecopoetics.

Understanding language poetry as complementary to ecopoetic theory is complicated by the variations in conceptions of both terms. While the term "ecopoetics" lacks a consistent meaning among its proponents, "language poetry" is similarly muddled, as it is used to refer to a wide array of poetic approaches. As Perloff explains, "the language movement has always been an umbrella for very disparate practices; moreover, now that it is over a decade old, it has, like any other movement, displayed internal conflicts and ruptures" (1991, 174). Some critics contend that language poetry is primarily about disjunction, while others argue that its connection to the reader constitutes language writing, and still others view it as a mode of politicized response to social issues. In "Re-thinking 'Non-retinal Literature': Citation, 'Radical Mimesis,' and Phenomenologies of Reading in Conceptual Writing," Judith Goldman attempts to prioritize the movement's concerns:

> Perhaps the most important commonality among Language poetries' strategies and self-understandings was the cultivation of de-reifying,

participatory forms of readership through the agency of disjunction and fragmentation. Fracturing words, syntax, and narrative diminishes extra-textual reference—a function that masks social control by presenting language as transparent—in favor of re-routing signifying processes to reveal oppressive social coding. (2011, par. 3)

According to major interpreters of language poetry, then, the movement's larger goal is to reveal the outside influences that impinge on conceptions and expressions of lived experience.

It is the shift toward lived experience that prompts many scholars of language writing to consider the subjective experiences of both the reader and writer in the movement. In *The Marginalization of Poetry: Language Writing and Literary History*, for instance, Bob Perelman observes that "language writing is best understood as a group phenomenon, and…one whose primary tendency is to do away with the reader as a separable category" (1996, 31). Anticipating Perelman in his essay "The Politics of, the Politics In," Jed Rasula, a scholar who has since worked extensively on ecopoetics,[5] contends that language writing is compelled toward restoring the reader as a participant in creating the text and emphasizes the material presence of objects (1987, 319). Pointing toward the role that the reader plays in shaping a text *and* the importance of the material or physical, both Perelman and Rasula emphasize language writing's destabilization of complete and objective poetic expression. When we recognize that the reader's subjective experience of the text plays a significant role and couple that with the poet's effort to express both natural and unnatural material objects or experiences on the page, the potential of an unnatural ecopoetic critique of language poetry can be clearly seen. Through this lens, the variety of elements that shape not only the reader but, perhaps more importantly, also influence the writer, move to the fore.

Critical examinations of language writing and poetry reveal that it is not as far removed from ecopoetic theory as might initially appear. In fact, many of the tenets of language poetry are remarkably similar to more recent trends in new materialisms, discussed in this book's introduction, which are central to the unnatural ecopoetic theory I propose. Serpil Oppermann gestures toward the connections that might exist between these seemingly disparate fields in "Theorizing Material Ecocriticism: A Diptych":

The old conceptions of matter as stable, inert, and passive physical substance, and of the human agent as a separate observer always in control, are being replaced here by the new posthumanist models that effectively theorize matter's inherent vitality. In ecological postmodern terminology, we are witnessing a "re-enchantment" of nature, and material ecocriticism is a significant contributor to this new paradigm. Evidently, it is the primary ecocritical expression of postmodern materialism. Examining how matter and meaning, bodies and texts, perception and experience intra-act with cultural productions and social systems, material ecocriticism becomes important as a heuristic model of postmodern materialism.[6] (Iovino and Oppermann 2012, 465)

Here, Oppermann posits that new materialisms, more specifically material ecocriticism, are changing perspectives of the physical world or matter by recognizing that the physical and the cultural ("matter and meaning, bodies and texts, perception and experience") are intertwined to the point that they are indistinguishable from one another. Although it is not the purpose of this chapter to outline new materialisms or material ecocritical theory, triangulating new materialisms with language poetry and ecopoetics reveals that naturalcultural intra-action is changing the direction of contemporary poetry criticism and perhaps even inspiring radical new forms that are more capable of accommodating it.[7] An unnatural ecopoetic examination of Hejinian's poetics will show that new materialist ideas about naturalcultural intra-action push up against language poetry's self-awareness and textual play, an interaction that facilitates the creation of new textual spaces that are capable of expressing naturalcultural environments on the page.

## HEJINIAN'S POETICS

Hejinian's work has long demonstrated a profound interest in language and form, but she also enters into an examination of materiality, discovering that experiences are shaped through the interactions of various elements rather than by any single element in isolation. Throughout her career, she has always been suited to the kind of unnatural ecopoetic critique proposed here, but some of her work, especially *My Life*, makes her connections between such diverse elements as personal experience, language, and form most apparent. In this sense, the poet's work illustrates how language poetry, new materialisms, and ecopoetics converge. Hejinian retrospectively gestures toward such a reading of her work when she writes in *The Language of Inquiry* that "the incapacity of language to match the world permits us to distinguish our ideas and ourselves from the world and things in it from each other. The undifferentiated is one mass, the differentiated is multiple" (2000, 56). For the poet, the limitations of language, the facet of her poetics that aligns her with the language poetry movement, are precisely what allow objects and events in the physical realm to become knowable. It is the interaction of world and word that facilitates being. In other words, through language's interaction with the world it purports to express, things are "differentiated" and attain individuality. As I recognize that the poet uses new materialist ideas and draws from her roots in language poetry in order to better express lived experience, I propose that unnatural ecopoetics provides an apt tool for Hejinian scholarship.

While an unnatural ecopoetic lens is well suited to *My Life*, Hejinian contends that she began moving toward the materially infused poetics even earlier. She explains that her first book, *Writing Is an Aid to Memory* (1978), explores how "language gives structure to awareness. And in doing so it blurs, and perhaps even effaces, the distinction between subject and object, since language is neither, being intermediate between the two" (2000, 23). Here, the poet expresses a clear interest in subject/object relations, and by exploring language and time in this early book, she examines the breakdown of any clear "distinction between subject and object," an interest that comes to fruition in *My Life*. Yet, the breakdown of subject and object that language facilitates is vital in her first book. *Writing Is an Aid to Memory* is an open-form text divided into forty-two sections, each of variable length and with lines that stagger from the left margin without any consistent pattern. The poem, perhaps even more so than Hejinian's subsequent work, is radically disjointed and defies any sense of development or connection from one line to the next and often even between words in the same line. As such, the book's form and content call into question fixed structures, like language and narrative, as it disrupts typical patterns and defies comprehension.

Perhaps even more significantly, though, *Writing Is an Aid to Memory* reflects on its own form by revealing precisely how and why the poet resists the limitations of traditional language use and how that resistance is related to her engagement with the material world. Although sprinkled throughout the book and deeply encoded in the text, her self-reflexive commentary is most apparent in the final section, when she writes:

              sign can't be justified in the slaughter<br>
        in this line basket rake in logic sort done until<br>
    deaths bore do obstacle to<br>
      I study is material<br>
              thoughtfulness collage bit river<br>
              the test apple bank as material think is<br>
              sense difference later differ doubt the<br>
              shape

> as night scratches understanding never wishes
> > > nothing is and no-one is beyond compare because
> > > never satisfied
> > brain badly rake harmless second done from my head to my
> > chest
> > > > where wishes are shot
> > > I differ the river to be torn six thing except
> > > is kept
> > > > > spent
> > > > > rake material
> > > > > scratch the poor in slaughter
> > > > > terrific river beats looking first to
> be
> > > > of partial length the awful ring of the familiar
> > > > torn in the second a doubt
> > > I am composed of human limbs until no longer capable
> > > of nature
>
> > > > > > > (1996, section 42)

The jumbled lines and disjointed sentiments of this section are representative of the book as a whole, leaving the reader unable to connect thoughts from one line to the next. However, this section engages in a somewhat sustained examination of language and materiality as it considers the "slaughter" performed by the imposition of the "sign." In this Saussurean reference, the speaker contends that the "sign can't be justified" in imposing "logic" and order to the point that the original object or experience becomes irrelevant ("until / deaths bore"). The passage turns instead to the "material" as she outlines the differences between "thoughtfulness" and to "think," proposing that "thoughtfulness" combines various elements and grants them equal agency ("thoughtfulness collage bit river / the test apple bank as material"), whereas to "think" is to impose order and categorization by dividing elements from one another ("think is / sense difference later differ doubt the / shape"). Privileging the noun over the verb, the speaker presents the former as cohesive and inclusive whereas the latter is intrusive and divisive. The divisiveness persists as she comments on "the river" and the "terrific river beats" of it being "torn" apart by "the ring of the famil-iar," a reference that might be tied to the appearance of the speaker's human-ity in the following lines. It is the human push for understanding, logic, and categorization—the verb "thinking"—that distances her from the river and nature altogether ("I am composed of human limbs until no longer capable / of nature"). The speaker's realization in this passage is a moment of self-reflection on the book itself, which detaches itself from the limitations of human logic and thought by discarding the need for "familiar" narrative structure or even comprehension. *Writing Is an Aid to Memory*, then, demonstrates an inclusive "thoughtfulness," in which multiple elements of place and experience are preserved and permitted to intra-act free of artificially imposed connection or detachment.

Not only in this early work but throughout her career, Hejinian's poetics balances between an effort to express the multiplicity that constitutes real-world experience and an impulse to reveal the inability of the text to ever fully express such openness. In *The Language of Inquiry*, she explains that her methodology emerges from the realization that humans are plagued "by the struggle between language and that which it claims to depict or express, by our overwhelming experience of the vastness and uncertainty of the world, and by what often seems to be the inadequacy of the imagination that longs to know it—and, furthermore, for the poet, the even greater inadequacy of the language that appears to describe, discuss, or disclose it" (2000, 49). In her quest for the radically open poem,[8] the poet contends with the complexity of experience and the expression of that multifaceted encounter in text. In essence, then, the poet's work is grounded in a naturalcultural struggle to textually express the intra-actions that constitute the experiences of everyday life. Although the coming pages will consider how this sentiment lies at the heart of Hejinian's most famous book, the naturalcultural impulse that drives unnatural ecopoetic readings of her work is evident in one of her most recent books, *Happily* (2000), which, Bob Perelman argues, has the single message "that things exist, person-size, sentence-size" (quoted in Hejinian, *Happily*, 2000, back cover). The overt materiality at the heart of Hejinian's small, thirty-nine-page book reveals how her earlier attempts, in *My Life* and elsewhere, to bring together natural, cultural, personal, and textual aspects of experience are grounded in both an interest in experience as multidimensional and an examination of language's ability to preserve that complexity. Unnatural ecopoetics exposes these poetic moves as naturalcultural approaches to lived experience.

An unnatural ecopoetic reading makes evident that in *Happily* the speaker's lived experiences remain present, but the text is overrun with an abundance of self-reflexive commentary on the nature of experience. Examining the multiplicity of lived encounters throughout, the book engages with Hejinian's concept of the "open text" on a highly theoretical level and perhaps more fully than in any of her previous books. In one of the most overt examples of this self-reflection, the speaker contemplates the materiality of experience in relation to the subjective factors that shape it:

The experiences generated by sense perception come by the
        happenstance that is with them
Experiences resulting from things impinging on us
There is continuity in moving our understanding of them as
        they appear
Some which are games bring with them their own rules for
        action which is a play we play which we may play with an
        end we value not winning
The dilemmas in sentences form tables of discovery of
        things created to create the ever better dilemma which
        is to make sense to others
    . . . . . . . . . . . . . . . . . . . .

Happinesses are not events that not a time can be taken for
States of intuition may be only sudden
*Now* is a blinding instant one single explosion but somehow
        some part of it gets accentuated
And each time the moment falls the emphasis of the moment
        falls into time differently

                                (2000, 26–27; emphasis in original)

In this passage, the speaker expresses both a profound interest in materiality and a preoccupation with language's ability to express it. The passage's engagement with materiality is reminiscent of the previous discussion of *Writing Is an Aid to Memory*, as it grants agency to things and embraces the diverse elements that compose experience. By connecting the "experiences" of "sense perception" with the "happenstance" that accompanies them, the speaker initiates a closer examination of the reality of lived experience. Realizing that "[e]xperiences" result from "things impinging on us" and require continual adjustment to integrate new "things" or happenstances ("There is continuity in moving our understanding of them as they appear"), she asserts that often those "things" change the experience altogether ("Some which are games bring with them their own rules for action which is a play we play"). Read through the lens of unnatural ecopoetics, this passage suggests that material objects or "things" outside of the human body are granted agency as they "impinge" on the human. Responding to the materiality of experience a few lines later, she states that "[h]appinesses are not events" that can be quantified and stabilized, but feelings ("States of intuition") that are instantaneous. In fact, these feelings are overwhelmingly complex and multiple, so much so that the speaker states that the moment is "a blinding instant one single explosion."

The unnatural ecopoetic critique becomes particularly relevant for this passage when it becomes evident that the material and nonmaterial elements of experience are tied up with an examination of the words that seek to express the encounter. As the speaker acknowledges that experiences are multiple and accompanied by peripheral, often irrelevant data or "happenstance," she turns to the role of writing in expressing that complexity. Claiming that "[t]he dilemmas in sentences form tables of discovery of things," the speaker comments on the ways that writing organizes the chaos of "happenstance" into "tables" or categories that facilitate understanding. Put another way, through writing the overwhelming is made perceptible. In *Poetic Investigations: Singing the Holes in History*, Paul Naylor contends that, for Hejinian, "restlessness manifests itself in the signifying process—not as an aberrational breakdown but as a constitutive activity: an activity revealing that language, like the text and like the self, is an event rather than an object" (1999, 136). As such, even as the speaker concludes that the moment is overwhelming and blinding in its complexity, she concedes that writing makes sense of the overwhelming instant by recording it in time ("each time the moment falls the emphasis of the moment falls into time differently"). *Happily*, then, is a poetic space where the material and nonmaterial elements of real-world experience are thrust together with the limitations of language as the poet attempts to navigate both simultaneously. As we have seen from her earlier work, this is a thread that runs throughout Hejinian's poetics but becomes more overt in this later text. In a sense, the unnatural ecopoetics in the poet's work is methodologized in *Happily*, as she overtly comments both on the materiality of lived experience and the limitations inherent in her own language and form while simultaneously exploring those limits through text.

## THE UNNATURAL ECOPOETICS OF *MY LIFE*

In her comments on *My Life*, Hejinian states that the text "gives the impression that it begins and ends arbitrarily and not because there is a necessary point of origin or terminus, a first or last moment. The implication (correct) is that the words and the ideas (thoughts, perceptions, etc.—the materials) continue beyond the work. One has simply stopped because one has run out of units or minutes, and not because a conclusion has been reached nor 'everything' said" (2000, 47). The poet's engagement with this philosophy is apparent through the publication history of *My Life*, as the book evolves and gains complexity in multiple versions that have appeared throughout the poet's life. The book was first published in 1980, when Hejinian was thirty-seven years old, and consisted of thirty-seven sections of thirty-seven sentences each. In 1987, the poet released an updated version that contained forty-five sections of forty-five sentences, corresponding to her age at the time. Finally, in 2003, Hejinian released *My Life in the Nineties*, a reiteration of the earlier texts' information from the perspective of the more aged poet.[9] The changes in the book's form are reminiscent of the poet's own claim that "words" and "ideas" develop and "continue beyond the work." In essence, *My Life* performs the poet's life as closely as possible by evolving with her, and this mimetic statement is a connection between word and world that the text struggles to both challenge and embrace.

In most readings of *My Life*, the evolving structure of the text is viewed in relation to language, form, and genre. Scholarship on the book considers everything from its interest in how language represents physical reality and form expresses the dynamism of lived experience to its relationship to autobiography. Approaches to the book from the perspective of language are common largely as a result of Hejinian's well-known connections to the language movement and as a result of the text's unusual prose form, which is often linked to language writing. For instance, Naylor articulates such a critical perspective through what he identifies as "restlessness" in the book. He contends that "restlessness manifests itself in the signifying process—not as an aberrational breakdown but as a constitutive activity: an activity revealing that language, like the text and like the self, is an event rather than an object" (Naylor 1999, 136). Considering how the text's form relates to its larger commentary on the relationship between language and material reality, Naylor's approach is representative of a large swath of scholarship on *My Life*. For some critics, though, like Megan Simpson, the link between language and lived experience is more prominent in the book. She observes that for Hejinian, "context, including language, is constitutive of all knowing. Since what we know and how we know can never be separated from the *process of knowing*, objective, final knowledge—scientific certainty—can never be secured. Some uncertainty or doubt will always remain" (Simpson 2000, 15; emphasis in original). For both Simpson and Naylor, language is central in the book because of its inevitable commentary on the gaps between perception, understanding, and expression.

In alternatives to the dominant approach of investigating language in the text, some critics consider how the text's autobiographical roots are significant to readings of it. In *Procedural Form in Postmodern American Poetry*, David Huntsperger clearly articulates the important role of the book's generic connections to autobiography: "We have, then, an interesting formal problem: a procedural poem that foregrounds the autobiographical origins of its constraints even as it subverts the conventions of autobiography" (2010, 132). He argues that the poem's procedural form coupled with its "autobiographical origins" facilitate the book's upheaval of the genre of autobiography, making such sentiments a central concern of the book. Similarly to Huntsperger, in "The Mnemonics of Autobiography: Lyn Hejinian's *My Life*," Hilary Clark contends that the nuances of the poem are linked to its commentary on autobiography. She argues, "*My Life* challenges the view that the events of a life form an ordered sequence culminating in an always-foreseen fullness of being—the writer's present life and vocation" (1991, 316). For Clark, the book's central purpose is to challenge the assumption so prominent in most autobiographies that events unfold chronologically. Approaches to Hejinian's text from the perspective of autobiography reveal that the book's unique challenge to the conventions of a popular genre might reflect its larger interest in challenging other fixed forms and boundaries.

An unnatural ecopoetic reading of *My Life* builds on earlier approaches to the text by reiterating that Hejinian's autobiography is atypical of its genre in challenging standard characteristics, including a chronological structure and clear narrative, and, more importantly, because she foregrounds the inability of her words to accurately depict the original event and instead attempts to mimic her own subjective, fragmented, and disjointed experience of the event's multiplicity on the page. As the poet explains, "In the gap between what one wants to say (or what one perceives there is to say) and what one can say (what is sayable), words provide for a collaboration and a desertion. We delight in our sensuous involvement with the materials of language, we long to join words to the world—to close the gap between ourselves and things—and we suffer from doubt and anxiety because of our inability to do so" (Hejinian 2000, 56). Including the many memories, tangents, physical sensations, and distractions that composed the event itself, her text demonstrates a tendency—prominent in my unnatural ecopoetic method—to preserve the chaotic non-narrative that dominates real-world experience. As unnatural ecopoetics reveals, humans do not experience only one sense or even one moment at a time, but are always overwhelmed with subjective distractions, such as memory and mental wandering, and the countless elements of the environment that, if not filtered, would confuse and overwhelm the perceiver. In *My Life*, though, the poet chooses not to filter her experiences but instead to maintain the fragmented, disjointed, and often confusing reality of them on the page.

The opening of *My Life* demonstrates the book's suitability to unnatural ecopoetic readings by emphasizing the many, often disjointed elements that contribute to one's perception of lived experiences and by turning toward the everyday fusion of multiple elements, ranging from material to emotional forces, that shape an encounter. From the beginning of the book, the poet thrusts memories and emotions from her own life into observations on the natural world, revealing the important influence of both the physical and the personal on experience. The book begins:

> A moment yellow, just as four years later, when my father returned home from war, the moment of greeting him, as he stood at the bottom of the stairs, younger, thinner than when he had left, was purple— though moments are no longer so colored. Somewhere, in the back-ground, rooms share a pattern of small roses. Pretty is as pretty does. In certain families, the meaning of necessity is at one with the sentiment of pre-necessity. The better things were gathered in a pen. The windows were narrowed by white gauze curtains which were never loosened. Here I refer to irrelevance, that rigidity which never intrudes. Hence, repetitions, free from all ambition. The shadow of the redwood trees, she said, was oppressive. The plush must be worn away. On her walks she stepped into people's gardens to pinch off cuttings from their gera-niums and succulents. An occasional sunset is reflected on the win-dows. A little puddle is overcast. (2002, 7)

In this opening passage the naturalcultural fusions of Hejinian's work are par-ticularly apparent. Drawing together elements of personal childhood mem-ories, adult reflection on them, contemplations on the nature of perception, commentary on writing, and a consideration of the supposed nature/culture gap, the speaker in this passage engages fully in a naturalcultural experience. The movement between these various elements is subtle, happening without warning and with rapid leaps from one moment or reflection to the next. The book remains true to its autobiographical genre by beginning with a gesture toward childhood perception as the speaker recounts a time in her life when moments were "colored" in "yellow" and "purple." Although she reveals that "moments are no longer so colored," or imbued with sensory perception, and implies that she grew out of that mode of perception, she bombards the reader with elements of the past both in their initial moment of occurrence, con-ceived through the limited perception of a small child, and as recounted from the perspective of an adult. Simpson contends that "the sense that something is always left out or glossed over in memory—that perfect knowledge of reality (in this case, the past as it 'really' was) is impossible—is a recurring, circulat-ing theme of this book-length, nonlinear, poetic work in prose" (2000, 12). In the opening lines, the fragmented memories of childhood that are seamlessly tied to the adult contemplation of them highlight the gaps between lived experiences and perceptions of them. The memory of her father returning "home from the war" is infused with the knowledge and understanding of the grown speaker, and thus the experience is irreversibly altered from its original form into something entirely new.

Following the inquiry into memory and perception in the opening lines, the passage engages with unnatural ecopoetic sentiments through its recognition of the interconnections between the human and nonhuman and its struggle to express those naturecultures on the page. Naturalcultural elements emerge when the speaker fuses the cultural concept of "rooms," or built structures that house, with the natural concept of "roses" when she proclaims that they share a pattern. The comparison is enhanced a few lines later when the speaker goes on to recall how "[t]he windows were narrowed by white gauze curtains which were never loosened." Here, the "rooms" are likened to "roses" but their counterpart, the "windows," are restricted by the "curtains" that permanently hang over them. In this sense, the rooms are permitted to share the pattern of the most culturally commodified flower, the "rose," but a clear view of the outside world is not permitted, being limited by the curtains. In this moment, the speaker comments on the human's inability to see entirely past the figurative curtains to the real world; put another way, she acknowledges that the human perceiver is always limited to human senses and never fully outside of the metaphorical house and the restrictions it imposes. Accepting this limitation, the speaker moves beyond a quest to bypass her human self and instead considers how elements in the natural world intertwine with her cultural space. As such, she does not turn to majestic images of nature but instead concludes that such a majestic image as "[t]he shadow of the redwood trees" is "oppressive" and instead looks to less grandiose and more everyday elements of nature that stem up in the garden ("cuttings from their geraniums and succulents"). The garden, a space where nature and culture fully intertwine through natural foliage organized in rigid cultural patterns, leads the speaker to acknowledge that naturalcultural elements emerge subtly in everyday life through moments and images like the reflection of the "occasional sunset" on the "windows" rather than through overt turns toward lofty images of nature.

Still, what makes Hejinian's text so uniquely suitable to unnatural ecopoetic readings, as opposed to broader materialist approaches, is her self-reflexive commentary, in which the limitations of the text are observed, recognized, and accepted rather than ignored or obfuscated. The movement in the opening passage of the book toward a naturalcultural sentiment is surrounded by commentary on poetic limitations. The speaker's observation that "[t]he better things were gathered in a pen," demands that the passage be considered in terms of writing, a move that prompts an unnatural ecopoetic critique rather than the more specialized but narrow material ecocritical reading. Stating that the "better" things are written implies a sense of hierarchy, in which some elements are more valuable and thus more worthy of writing than others. It might be assumed that her written family history is based on those moments that are considered "better" rather than on an accurate depiction of her life. However, the speaker turns in another direction when she proclaims that in this poem ("Here") she is turning to "irrelevance, that rigidity which never intrudes." As Simpson contends, Hejinian's work runs "counter to modes of knowing that value objectivity and certainty and that are bent on the acquisition of knowledge as something existing separate from and prior to the means of acquiring and categorizing that prize" (2000, 12). The "irrelevance" that she embraces in this moment is a turning away from prioritizing the "better things" over those not worthy of recording and toward a poem that allows for the irrelevance inherent in real-world experience and thus can minimally "intrude" or alter the original experience.

As the opening lines demonstrate, Hejinian's unnatural ecopoetic sentiments are clearly expressed through her overt use of self-reflexive commentary on writing in general as well as on the genre of autobiography. Acknowledging that the act of perception causes some change to the original experience, the poet embraces and foregrounds the limitations of her own form. Her focus on language is apparent throughout the book, but before considering how the poet approaches language it seems apt to consider the larger critique at the heart of the book—the critique of autobiography. Although many critics read the text as autobiography, *My Life* can be labeled so only in the loosest sense of the word. Unlike in traditional examples of the genre, the poet does not provide a clear depiction of the events of her life but instead presents a highly complex and largely incomprehensible series of observations, memories, thoughts, and influences. As Simpson observes, "Hejinian's poetics take the process, context, and materials of the knowing situation into account as components of the knowing itself, rather than trying to separate knowledge (as a product) from the process of 'acquiring' it" (2000, 16). In this way, the poet engages with the context of her life in a way that traditional autobiography does not. She acknowledges that her experiences are tied up in a series of elements, including natural and cultural ones that continually intertwine within her mind. As the poet explains, in *My Life* "the structural unit (grossly, the paragraph) was meant to be mimetic of both a space and a time of thinking" (Hejinian, 2000, 46). To separate one element out would be inauthentic to the experience because it attempts to isolate one facet of experience from another, a goal that *My Life* presents as impossible.

In the book, each sentence is tied to the next not through a clear narrative but through a surprisingly seamless flow from one unrelated thought or observation to the next. The reader is not compelled to continue reading because of an investment in the narrative itself but through a power to piece together the events for him or herself. Juliana Spahr contends that the power that the reader holds in interpreting Hejinian's book is precisely what gives the text such a unique ability to express the true nature of experience. She claims that in "*My Life*, an attention to a larger world is accompanied by a move to share authority with readers and an accompanying abandoning of authorial privilege" (2001, 53). Hejinian's background in language poetry is apparent, as she grants power to the reader to shape the text. Aside from the politically charged roots that such moves have in language poetry, granting the reader authority to interpret and shape the text works ecopoetically. Once the reader is granted freedom and authority to insert him or herself into the text, the apparent subjectivity of the writer becomes balanced by the subjective experience of the reader. The author's experiences are evaluated and critiqued for their authenticity and recognized for their limitations. As such, the experience of reading the text is as important as the experience of writing it because it allows the text to remain active and flexible to the encounter it seeks to express. The importance of subjectivity in *My Life* is apparent when the speaker states: "There were more storytellers than there were stories, so that everyone in the family had a version of history and it was impossible to get close to the original, or to know 'what really happened'" (2002, 27). The "storytellers" identified in the passage are certainly the poet's family but are also tied to the way the text reveals itself and the events it reconstitutes. Naylor explains this by stating that for Hejinian, "restlessness manifests itself in the signifying process—not as an aberrational breakdown but as a constitutive activity: an activity revealing that language, like the text and like the self, is an event rather than an object" (1999, 136). The autobiography does not function for the poet as a simple depiction of events but rather as a flexible space in which an event slowly unfolds in the highly disjointed way that lived encounters reveal themselves. In other words, Hejinian's autobiography captures the material and nonmaterial elements that constitute her real-world experience and expresses them in the foregrounded textual space of the poem. When read through the lens of unnatural ecopoetics, then, the book is seen to be engaging in a complex rendering of experience that includes the many disjointed and peripheral elements that are often overlooked or discarded in textual renderings of lived experiences.

The poet's use of autobiography may initially seem to run counter to the concept of ecopoetics in general. But her willingness to embrace naturalcultural elements through her complex "open text" and preserve all facets of her experiences makes her seemingly self-absorbed and entirely anthropocentric autobiographical poem more authentic to a real-world experience, which is always infused with elements from the past, present, future, as well as with subjective wanderings into political, historical, environmental, and personal tangents. Still, to express such sentiments in the text the poet must consider not only the genre but also the medium in which she writes. Writing is a central point of concern throughout Hejinian's poetics. In *My Life* she continually articulates the challenges and limitations of writing through her use of self-reflexive statements, and she insists throughout the book that writing remain in the foreground. Writing acts as the center of the book because through it the poet explores what can and cannot be expressed in text. The speaker articulates the challenges of language subtly throughout. In one such instance, she emphasizes the limitations of words:

> The inaccessibility of the meaning intrigued me all the more, since I couldn't read the single letters, if that is what they were, the little marks which constitute Persian. Mother dimension; sex. She observed that detail minutely, as if it were botanical. As if words could unite an ardent intellect with the external material world. Listen to the drips. The limits of personality. It's in the nature of language to encourage, and in part to justify, such Faustian longings. Break them up into uncounted continuous and voluminous digressions. (2002, 63)

The speaker is intrigued by her inability to comprehend or "read" the "letters" or "little marks" before her because they are in "Persian." The "inaccessibility of the meaning," though, does not fascinate her only because of its foreignness; it intrigues her "more," implying an ongoing acceptance that meaning is always out of reach. However, the speaker's examination of language becomes most overt when she explains that the female "She" examines "detail minutely" as though she were examining plant life ("as if it were botanical"). Conflating the broad concept of detail with plants, the speaker goes on to explain that it is "as if words could unite an ardent intellect with the external material world." Here, the text turns toward a pronounced self-reflexive statement as the speaker mocks the idea ("as if") that language can connect the human intellect to the physical world. Scoffing at the thought that words can somehow bridge this gap, the speaker instead proposes turning to the senses to access the "material world." She encourages the reader to "listen to the drips" and, in doing so, acknowledge the "limits" of the human mind ("intellect" and "personality"). Ultimately, she asserts that it is "the nature of language" to encourage the accessibility or comprehension promised by the intellect, but if one listens to the sounds of the world in their many disjointed parts rather than trying to understand them ("Break them up into uncounted continuous and voluminous digressions"), then the senses take control and move beyond the demand for comprehension, logic, and accessibility.

The speaker's turn toward promoting the experiences of the senses over the limitations of logic and meaning are an attempt to preserve the inaccessibility of lived experience. Naylor argues that "*My Life*, by drawing attention to the limits of language, draws attention to the limits of logic and, more significantly, to the fictive element in the process that produces both language and logic—the signifying process" (1999, 123). Much as the speaker in this passage is overwhelmed by the inaccessible foreignness of the words before her, the human observer is constantly overcome by the sensations, elements, thoughts, memories, and emotions that constitute a lived experience. It is only when one ceases to search for understanding and instead embraces the disjointed reality of real-world encounters that he or she can truly access those moments. In terms of writing, words are presented in this passage as limiting. Similarly, in a later section, the speaker again turns toward the senses when logic and reason fail to suffice, stating, "It's hard to make a heart go pal pal pal at description but with that fat music on big feet I go beat beat beat and twitch containment" (2002, 92). The "heart" does not beat for the logic or clarity of "description" but instead for the sensation of "music" that gets the listener on his or her "feet." The involvement of the perceiver and the activity of the senses intrigues the speaker, providing a means to engage with the world on a much deeper level than simple description can ever provide. In this sense, the speaker concludes that while logic brings accessibility and comprehension, it does not express the true nature of experience. The speaker's examination of the boundaries of logic and ultimately language here, then, exhibits Hejinian's poetics and shows how an unnatural ecopoetic reading that brings the various elements of her poetics together enlightens understandings of the text. Turning away from comprehensibility through radical formal and narrative experimentation, *My Life* embarks on a more sensory-driven journey on which experience remains realistically disjointed.

The unnatural ecopoetic sentiment that lies at the heart of Hejinian's poetics gains prominence throughout the text as the poet comments on the limitations of her own form, ultimately foregrounding the boundaries of the book. By highlighting those parameters, the speaker demonstrates to the reader her own awareness of them and allows the book's boundaries to remain visible throughout the text through constant reminders that a word can never equal the world. The speaker says that preserving those limitations is essential to escaping the pull toward the deceptive promises of comprehension, accessibility, and description that writing encourages:

> They used to be the leaders of the avant garde, but now they just want to be understood, and so farewell to them. If I was left unmarried after college, I would be single all my life and lonely in old age. In such a situation it is necessary to make a choice between contempt and an attempt at understanding, and yet it is difficult to know which is the form of retreat. We will only understand what we have already understood. (2002, 73)

Commenting on artists who "used to" be considered "avant garde" and radical but sacrificed their rebellion for the drive "to be understood," the speaker concludes that when faced with such a difficult choice between acceptance and comprehensibility, "we will only understand" those things that "we have already understood." That is, understanding is limiting because it does not evolve or expand but stays the same. She later comments that the restrictions imposed by logical meaning are so pronounced that they consume the original sensation they seek to express: "I remember my fear of personality, which was so similar to the fear of forgetting that the tiniest idea became a 'nagging thought,' until I could write it down and out, preserved, but, in a sense, too, eliminated" (2002, 131). Returning to the limits of personality from an earlier passage, the speaker reveals that her "fear of personality" causes her to fear losing thoughts. Out of that fear, she writes them down. What is perhaps most fascinating here, though, is that the act of recording or writing down the thoughts destroys them ("eliminated"). It is as though her attempt to record thought runs counter to the potential power of writing. In a sense, recording the thought is an attempt to preserve and make it accessible, but to do so, the writer must reduce the thought to the logic and limits of language.

The speaker's ongoing disparagement of language foregrounds the book's textuality and calls into question the ability of *My Life* to effectively express Hejinian's lived experience in its original form, as an autobiography traditionally aspires to do. Since the self-reflexive moments in the text reveal that language is largely limited and can destroy meaning, the poet's attempt to adapt her life to the page appears inherently flawed. However, it is the acknowledgment of those limits that facilitates the text's effectiveness and makes the book well suited to unnatural ecopoetic critique. Making the reader aware of her own dissatisfaction with the reach of language, the poet creates a text that is decidedly artificial but marked by elements of real-world experience. The speaker explains this unnatural ecopoetics through metacommentary on her own form:

> A paragraph is a time and place, not a syntactic unit. We stood watching circles in the light beside the lake, while in the last sunlight flew a mob of tiny bugs, like motes of dust, doubt, or the code of the trees. More and more lake is contained by the stone thrown into it. The voices of the daughter, the mother, and the mother of the mother are heard in the background, and to their scattered bodies go. So quoted, coded. Things are different but not separate, thoughts are discontinuous but not unmotivated (like a rose without a pause). (2002, 137)

The speaker asserts that the "paragraph" is both temporal and physical ("a time and place"), thus referential to real experience, and not purely textual ("not a syntactic unit"). In this moment, the book's unnatural ecopoetic sentiments are clearly revealed, as the textual space of the book is tied to the material environments that it depicts. While the speaker comments on the idyllic scene of the lake, she fuses the physical world with the textual when she comments on "the code of the trees" and the "quoted, coded" voices in the scene. Ultimately, she suggests that the text and the world are "different but not separate" and that a lack of continuity does not necessarily mean meaninglessness ("thoughts are discontinuous but not unmotivated"). Perelman argues that "while Hejinian's use of parataxis coexists more amiably with narrative, her sentences are also committed to breaking up any smooth narrative plane. De-narrativization is a necessary part of construction in these wider paratactic arguments" (1996, 78). Perelman views the formal elements of the book as a strategy for depicting the lived experience more accurately than pure description ever can. Extending his claim, I contend that unnatural ecopoetics reveals that the poet's text is more than a linguistic space; it is also imbued with the materiality of the world around it.

Hejinian's text is unique in its engagement with materiality, though, because it employs the material through the lens of inevitably subjective experience and within markedly limited modes of textual expression. In *My Life*, the boundaries of the poem are uncovered again and again, but the poet successfully triangulates the material with the limits of both perception and text through repetition. In fact, through one key phrase that repeats in various forms throughout the book, the poetics of *My Life* is revealed. The phrase, "a pause, a rose, something on paper," which recurs in a variety of forms and contexts, is only one of a number of repeated phrases, a choice that draws attention to both the inexactness of language and the inauthenticity of textual expression.[10] Yet, in this particular phrase the poet engages with the lived experience ("a pause"), a material object ("a rose"), and a textual space ("something on paper"), while simultaneously emphasizing, through the artificiality of repetition, the constructedness of language.

A closer look at the repeated phrase reveals that its triangulation of subjective experience, the material world, and text lends itself to unnatural ecopoetic critique because it foregrounds the limitations of perception in relation to the complexity of the material world. The influence of logic on perceptions of lived experience is a central theme throughout Hejinian's book, but in this key phrase the influence of human thought on the material object is exaggerated.[11] In its various forms, the phrase "a pause, a rose, something on paper" might be read as a direct commentary on the distortive influence of thought on the material object. Within the phrase, it seems that in the translation from material reality to text, the rose is transformed from its original self—the flower—to a nondescript "something." The leap from materiality to textuality is, then, interrupted or distorted, implying a lack of continuity between the two. Interestingly, the phrase "a pause" accompanies the translation and brings with it a hesitation in which human thought or perception takes hold. The "pause" stands in for the inevitable subjectivity of experience, in which thoughts begin to shape perceptions of the material and ultimately transform them into something textual but entirely changed. Huntsperger contends that the pause "alludes to some mental or physical act that precedes the perception of the subsequent objects" (2010, 144). The "pause" marks the moment that the "rose" is perceived, which forces all perceptions of the rose to be filtered through human thought. Put another way, the "pause" reveals the inability to ever fully escape the influence of human thought or logic and reveals the unavoidable gap between the material and the textual. As the material "rose" is perceived and adapted to language, it is no longer a rose but only "something on paper," which is unrecognizable not only as a rose but even as a flower.

Hejinian's repeated phrase is elucidated by an unnatural ecopoetic approach, which recognizes the importance of the poet's choice to foreground the text's constructedness. By integrating a phrase so deeply imbued with commentary on perception, text, and materiality into the book through dynamic repetition, the poet draws attention to the line and its reiteration in a variety of contexts. As it evolves into a number of other iterations, the phrase is tied to questions about human perceptions of nature ("A pause, a rose, something on paper, in a nature scrapbook"), the inescapability of perception, materiality, and text ("I found myself dependent on a pause, a rose, something on paper"), and the boundaries of textual expression ("A pause, a rose, something on paper implicit in the fragmentary text") (2002, 16, 28, 55). By repeating the phrase through various iterations, the poet forces the reader to contend with the multiplicity inherent in each word and the various ways in which those words might be contextualized. In doing so, the words themselves are revealed as fragile and flexible. For Hejinian, the inexactness of language is always dominant, but it is the recognition of its limits that allows it to function. By foregrounding the text's artificial construction, the poet is able to better express the multiple ways in which experience is perceived by human observers and adapted to text. Hejinian's unnatural ecopoetics, then, emerges most explicitly through the repetition in the book, which foregrounds textual artificiality while self-reflexively exploring both those boundaries of the text and the relationship between subjective relations and lived experience and the material world.

### CONCLUSION

*My Life* is an unusual text to consider through the lens of unnatural ecopoetics because it is tied to the genre of autobiography, which is characterized by unembellished narrative, chronological structures, and engagement with the subjective experiences of the author. However, it is precisely its concern with the relation between the human, the world, and language that makes Hejinian's autobiography not only suitable but ideal for unnatural ecopoetic readings. Through this lens readers become aware that the book's unique style and apparent disregard for the conventions of autobiography facilitate an unusual self-awareness through which inadequate renderings of lived experience are accepted and appreciated for their shortcomings because their inadequacy reveals the gaps between the lived moment, human perception, and textual expression. For the poet, only by embracing such a chasm and foregrounding it in the text can a poem begin to express something meaningful. In *The Language of Inquiry*, Hejinian asks, "Can form make the primary chaos (the raw material, the unorganized impulse and information, the uncertainty, incompleteness, vastness) articulate without depriving it of its capacious vitality, its generative power?...In my opinion, the answer is yes; that is, in fact, the function of form in art. Form is not a fixture but an activity" (2000, 47). These words run like a vein throughout *My Life*, as the poet's formal experimentation leads to a text that is utterly true to the disjointed, fragmentary, and multiplicitous nature of lived experiences in the world precisely because of its self-awareness and acceptance of its own inadequacy.

In this way, Hejinian's poetics stands as an example of the necessity of unnatural ecopoetics, a mode of reading that considers both her formal experimentation and her self-reflexive commentary. While other approaches to her work acknowledge some facet of her writing, such as language or form, unnatural ecopoetics allows for a more complete analysis of her poetry. Through this lens, readers can begin to recognize the poet's nuanced engagement with material and nonmaterial elements that influence experiences both at the moment of their occurrence and for the adult poet recalling them. Such a reading shows that unnatural ecopoetics presents new directions for poetry scholarship, as it allows readers to consider a poet's formal and linguistic play along with more personal reflections on memory and experience. This new brand of ecopoetics recognizes that lived experience is complex, multiple, and often inexpressible but attempts to interact and at least partially express these otherwise inexpressible encounters by approaching them from multiple directions at once. Such an approach opens doors to poets like Hejinian, who have previously been pigeonholed in one school or another and allows their work to be read with a more balanced look at the nuances of their poetics. As my reading of Hejinian's complex poetics demonstrates, expressing lived experience on the page is a constant struggle with language, form, experience, and self that unnatural ecopoetics helps to decipher.

### NOTES

1. The essay "The Rejection of Closure" was published in Hejinian's collection of essays *The Language of Inquiry* in 2000 but grew out of a version published in Bob Perelman's *Writing/Talks* in 1985. A version of the essay was also given as a talk in 1983 (Hejinian, 2000, 40).

2. Hejinian writes, "A central activity of poetic language is formal. In being formal, in making form distinct, it opens—makes variousness and multiplicity and possibility articulate and clear" (2000, 56). Her concept of multiplicity of experience is central to unnatural ecopoetics.

3. *My Life* was originally published in 1980, and a longer version appeared in 1987. Additionally, the poet released an updated and even longer version entitled *My Life in the Nineties* in 2003.

4. In "Language Poetry and Collective Life," Oren Izenberg explains that language poetry was "conceived as a response to two roughly contemporaneous if incommensurable developments—the American government's involvement in the Vietnam War and the American university's enthusiastic reception of continental literary theory" (2003, 132). Similarly, Reinfeld writes that "language poets operate as both politically and philosophically oriented intellectuals" (1992, 3).

5. See Rasula's book *This Compost: Ecological Imperatives in American Poetry* (2002). In a sense, Rasula links, albeit loosely, his early discussion of language writing with ecopoetics when he writes that "poetry is this strangely familiar realm of estrangements, its uncanniness preternaturally arousing a maximum alertness, but an alertness achieved paradoxically, by

dissolving the resources of intellection and identity" (2002, 8). Still considering the disorientation of the poem, a disjunction arguably rooted in language writing, he contends that such poetic approaches allow the individual to distance him or herself from the imposition of logic that might skew the material object or experience.

6. This article is cowritten by Oppermann and Serenella Iovino, but the passage quoted here comes from a section written exclusively by Oppermann.

7. The term "intra-action" is taken from Karen Barad's *Meeting the Universe Halfway*, in which she explains that "'intra-action' signifies the mutual constitution of entangled agencies. That is, in contrast to the usual 'interaction,' which assumes that there are separate individual agencies that precede their interaction, the notion of intra-action recognizes that distinct agencies do not precede, but rather emerge through, their intra-action" (2007, 33).

8. See Hejinian's essay "The Rejection of Closure" in *The Language of Inquiry* for a complete discussion of her concept of the open text (2000).

9. In this chapter, I will be working with the Green Integer reprint of the 1987 edition because it is the most widely referenced and read version of the text.

10. There are a large number of repeated phrases throughout the book (aside from the one discussed at length in this chapter), which range from references to those who "love to be astonished" to observations that "it is hard to turn away from moving water" to claims that "the obvious analogy is with music."

11. The poet's struggle with the ways in which human logic alters original events is apparent throughout the book but is perhaps most prominently displayed in her consideration of the standard calendar in relation to the "Mayan calendar," which "has more days" (2002, 55). In this scene, the speaker documents the artificiality of logical structures such as time by highlighting their breakdown through the simple act of turning to an alternative epistemological structure, such as the "Mayan calendar." In doing so, the speaker implies that logical systems, which seem incontrovertible, are easily destabilized.

# [ 3 ]

## Toward Textual Space in Susan Howe's
## *The Midnight*

*I am assembling materials for a recurrent return somewhere.*
*Familiar sound textures, deliverances, vagabond*
*quotations, preservations, wilderness shrubs, little*
*resuscitated patterns. Historical or miraculous.*
*Thousands of correlations have to be sliced and spliced.*

—SUSAN HOWE, *The Midnight*

SUSAN HOWE's *The Midnight* weaves together various aspects of culture, history, physical space, and genealogy in a collage that highlights middle spaces, but the poem's fusions also project the import of material and nonmaterial aspects of a spatial experience, including natural and unnatural elements alike. *The Midnight* brings these elements together as it engages in formal and linguistic inquiries into the ability of language to accurately express the often divergent facets of material experience. Despite its interest in the material, the book has not been widely read as an ecopoem because it employs history, memory, imagination, and physical encounter as well as a fractured, experimental form in order to convey the disjointed reality of experience, in which past and present are often simultaneously thrust together in the mind. Unnatural ecopoetics, though, reasserts these divergent elements of real-world encounters. Through this lens, which engages with the nuances of Howe's poetics directly, the poet's subtle self-reflexive commentary, experimental formal structures, and integration of found text work to construct a textual space that expresses a complex material experience. In other words, although the poem jumps between a variety of material spaces and nonmaterial thoughts, memories, histories, and reflections, making its environment unstable throughout, Howe constructs a foregrounded textual environment that captures the multiplicity and simultaneity of experience.

*The Midnight* is best described as a collage that brings together elements of the poet's personal life, peripheral historical data, linguistic inquiry, and formal play through a generic mingling of prose, poetry, and visual arts. The book is divided into five clearly marked sections, each of which takes on a new form as it jumps back and forth between the three genres. As in most of Howe's books, there is little continuity between lines, words, and even passages, seemingly begging the readers to accept disjunction and confusion but simultaneously prompting them to continue through traces of meaning and connection that sporadically emerge and disappear into the text. Although these disjunctions lead many critics to read Howe's work as language poetry, in much the same vein as Hejinian, and recognize it for its inquiries into historical and cultural peripheries, the collage that constitutes her writing ties the poet not only to the various included elements but also to an investigation into the boundaries of language and the physical world. In *The Midnight*, in particular, the material domineers and even shapes the formal dimensions of the book as physical objects and real-world events are inserted into the poetic space through meanderings into the poet's personal life, historical references, and photographs of everything from book pages to portraits; however, these elements spark nonmaterial reflection from the poet, who consistently ties the material aspects of experience to her subjective encounters with them. Chapter 2 demonstrated that Hejinian's poetics foregrounds the physicality of words; the following chapter on the conceptual poetry of Goldsmith argues that he features the agential power of textual space. Howe's writing stands between the two, as it foregrounds the materiality of text and textuality of the physical world simultaneously.

The depth of Howe's interest in space often goes unnoticed and unexamined in scholarship on her work, tempering ecocritical enthusiasm for the poet.[1] The revelations of material ecocriticism that are brought to the fore through unnatural ecopoetics, however, show that when environments are understood not only as natural places but as spaces composed of a particular perceiver's subjective experience of how physical, mental, emotional, textual, and political elements come together to compose an experience in time and space, Howe's poetics emerges as an unlikely but apt site for ecocritical study. Through the lens of unnatural ecopoetics, readers will recognize a new thread in Howe's complex poems and can begin to consider not only how her poems comment on text and poetry but also how they reflect on the complex nature of experience in the world.

## HOWE'S POETICS

As her career has developed from its origins in visual arts and theater toward an elaborate textual poetics, Howe's work has been read for everything from its feminist undertones to its historical recordings to its formal techniques.

Despite the poet's objection, many critics identify her as a language poet because of her radically experimental forms, while others highlight her prominent fascination with history.[2] Marjorie Perloff, Paul Naylor, Rachel Tzvia Back, and Peter Quartermain have specifically analyzed Howe's poetics in its many forms, each illustrating that the poet's work demands different theoretical lenses. For most critics working on Howe, the extreme ambiguity and radical experimentation of her writing provoke the reader toward interpretation, a process that not only enhances a poem's meaning but requires it. And for many scholars, including Lyn Keller, Howe's work engages with history and memory in an effort to draw out the underrepresented voices within it. Keller observes that Howe's "writing embodies absence in its elliptical and disjunctive character, and in its dramatic use of space on the page. Absence is a thematic preoccupation as well, particularly in Howe's concern with voices that have been silenced, figures who have been erased" (Keller 1995, 1). Keller's reading demonstrates a fairly common conception of the poet's work as primarily concerned with history and memory. However, Howe's writing also garners attention for its concern with landscape or place, concepts that seem particularly foreign to her highly formalized avant-garde poetry. Certainly, history and memory as well as formal experimentation play vital roles in her poetics, but the poet's interest in landscape is obscured by layers of cultural, personal, and historical exploration that dramatically alter material spaces.

Considering its muted role within the texts, material space is recognized in a surprising amount of Howe criticism. For instance, in *Led by Language: The Poetry and Prose of Susan Howe*, Back contends that the poet's personal and family history have made her more aware of the important role that environments play in determining personhood and facilitating belonging (2002, 9). Commenting both on the poet's unique formal techniques and her engagement with place, Back considers place a central element in the poet's engagement with personal and cultural history. It is through place that the poet is able to examine her own histories. Critics like Naylor, though, view landscape as a much more contentious site in Howe's work. In *Poetic Investigations: Signing the Holes in History*, he describes her work as engaging with the inability of poetry to ever express an unimpeded interaction with landscape and emphasizing the inability of words to shed their connotations (1999, 54). His reading argues that landscape and language in the poet's work are deeply embedded in cultural, political, historical, and personal systems.

Yet, even when the poet's engagement with landscape is noticed, it is not often granted adequate importance; most studies minimize the landscape's influence in her work or the deep level at which her poetics is embedded within environments. The notable exception is Scott Knickerbocker's limited treatment of Howe in the concluding chapter of his book, where he posits that Howe's *Articulation of Sound Forms in Time* presents "language as itself wild, part of nature broadly conceived" (2012, 175). Although Howe serves only as a concluding example in Knickerbocker's book, his reading raises important questions about the ways in which the poet engages with environments—both material and textual. Additionally, his recognition of the importance of sound for Howe gestures toward a connection between sound and space that seems central to some of the poet's recent work.

In fact, her 2010 book *That This* reveals that the poet views environments as multidimensional, including text, visual images, sounds, and lived encounter. Although the book's fragmented collage-style is relatively commonplace in the body of Howe's work, her 2011 collaboration with composer David Grubbs emphasizes the environmental experience of her poetry in an entirely new way. The work, entitled *Frolic Architecture*, after the second section of Howe's *That This*, blends the poet's readings of her poems with word fragments, ambient noise, and music, creating a layered effect in which the text of the poems blends with other elements of the experience, almost embodying the photograms by James Welling that accompany Howe's poems in the book. The *Frolic Architecture* project emphasizes the importance of sound, space, and experience in Howe's work.

However, the predominance of space is not new in her work. Looking back at her formal education in visual arts and her history in theater, it is clear that the poet has always been deeply embedded in a sort of unnatural ecopoetry that revolves around spatial experience. Howe presents an exciting new direction for unnatural ecopoetics because her work so prominently relies on and is rooted in visual arts, a mode that pulls powerfully away from traditional poetic practice and uses the methods of visual arts not to mimic, as in traditional ecopoetics, but to capture the multifaceted reality of experience. Her attention to landscape is, in many ways, tied to her roots in the art world. Trained in visual arts and theater, following her mother, Mary Manning, who was a famous Irish actress, Howe began her career in visual and performance arts, meandering into poetry through experiential art. In an interview conducted in 1994 by Lynn Keller, the poet explains the powerful roots of her poetics in visual art.

> Before we moved out of New York I had started making environments—rooms that you could walk into and be surrounded by walls, and one those walls would be collage, using found photographs (again a kind of quotation). Then I started using words with that work. I was

at the point where I was only putting words on the walls and I had
surrounded myself with words that were really composed lines when
a friend, the poet Ted Greenwald, came by to look at what I was doing
and said to me: "Actually you have a book on the wall. Why don't you
just put it into a book?" (quoted in Keller 1995, 6)

Reading the poet's work as tied to landscape appears apt; however, such readings may not attribute as much of her writing to place or environment as
Howe's poetic origins might warrant. For Howe, poetry began in art and, perhaps even more importantly, in environment. As an artist, she assembled
rooms of words, forcing her audience to physically enter a textual space as she
fused the real world with the poetic realm. Recognizing the photographs that
she placed on the walls as "a kind of quotation," and slowly building toward
increasing numbers of words, Howe's visual art engaged not only with the aesthetic but also with the experiential. The "environments" that she constructed
demanded physical engagement from the viewer as well as engagement with
visual, textual, and artistic spaces. Howe's artwork, then, employed much the
same process as her poetry—demanding the reader's involvement. It is only
when readers enter her artistic "environment" or the poem that they can begin
to contribute to its meaning. Bringing with them subjective interpretations,
memories, moods, aesthetic preferences, attention to detail, political penchants,
among other things, the viewers shape the experience of the art just as much
as the poet's subjective experience shapes the text. In this sense, the poet's artwork, like her poetry, asserts that one's subjective experience of place, or art, or
event shapes the project's meaning.

The poet's acknowledgment of how subjective experiences make for
diverse interpretations of real-world objects or events shows that she conceptualizes environments or places with more flexibility than most critics of her
work concede. Not viewing the environment as a purely physical phenomenon,
as her work in visual arts demonstrates, she presents environments as multiplicitous, composed of many objective and subjective elements at once. Her
conceptions of environment are perhaps most explicit in "Thorow," the poem
that gets the most attention for its use of landscape or place. The poem, whose
title derives from a phonetic spelling of Henry David Thoreau's name, begins
with clearly environmental undertones. Since Thoreau is widely viewed as a
father of environmental thought and sustainable living, Howe's engagement
with his legacy in this poem places particular attention on how she engages
with physical landscapes throughout her poetics. "Thorow" appears as the
second of three sections in Howe's 1990 collection, Singularities, and like much

of her other work, oscillates between prose and poetry while also varying line length and page layout. Some pages of the text contain numbered sections, some fill the page, some contain only a few lines, and some are scrambled across the page in various directions. According to Edward Allen in "'Visible Earshot': The Returning Voice of Susan Howe," the poem "enacts the encounter of a remembered self with the great outdoors—the Adirondacks, in this case—and in doing so gives voice to a 'transcendental subjectivity' in the first throes of linguistic disorientation" (2012, 402–3). Allen's critique argues that "Thorow" participates in much the same "disorientation" as the poet's other work. However, the origins of this text in one of the key figures of American transcendentalism and sustainability readily identifies it with a holistic concept of nature or environment that seems to run counter to the poet's use of landscape in other texts. Viewing nature as whole, pure, and revitalizing, the poem's evocation of Thoreau here is quite different from the highly fragmented landscapes or environments identified by other Howe scholars.

However, the poet's connection to Thoreau's experience of environment is her sense of dissolution into environment, where the human and natural become intertwined. In the poem, the speaker documents a journey through wilderness: "In March, 1987, looking for what is looking, I went down to unknown regions of indifferentiation. The Adirondacks *occupied* me" (Howe 1990, 40). Like Thoreau, the speaker here articulates a journey into the wild and "unknown" Adirondacks. What is perhaps most interesting about the setup of the speaker's entry into the wild is her fusion with the place, not only the human entering nature, but also nature entering the human ("Adirondacks *occupied* me"). In her article "The Landscapes of Susan Howe's 'Thorow,'" Jenny L. White identifies the poet's refusal to ignore naturalcultural influences, explaining that "Howe foregrounds conflict and works against a linear, narrative, or even coherent representation of place, in form as well as in content. The poem refuses to empty out the landscape it describes, to make it straightforward or a place of belonging; rather, it focuses on place as contested, particularly in terms of gender, race, and culture" (2006, 239). In this way, the poet sets up a unique encounter with the landscape, not only seeing and acting upon nature but allowing nature to act on the perceiver. Normally this aspect of Howe's poetics warrants little further consideration, but her naturalcultural sentiments in "Thorow" reveal a deeply rooted curiosity in how physical environments and cultural data coexist. Even in this earlier poem, then, an unnatural ecopoetic reading appropriately identifies the poet's fascination with preserving both natural and cultural elements of experience through the textual space.

Although not typically given much attention in scholarship on the poem, even that criticism that specifically considers landscape in "Thorow," Howe's relationship with nature is clearly one of interconnection and embeddedness. The poem further complicates this relationship when it adds language into considerations of nature.

> We go through the word Forest
>
> Trance of an encampment
> not a foot of land cleared
>
> The literature of savagism
> under a spell of savagism
>
> Nature isolates the Adirondacks
>
> In the machinery of injustice
> my whole being is Vision
>
> (1990, 49)

While the speaker's setup for the poem discussed in the previous paragraph remarks on the occupation of the perceiver by the place, this later section ties language to the complex experiences of landscape. The passage begins by explicitly conflating landscape and language, explaining that the poem brings the reader not "through" the "forest" itself, but through "the word Forest." In this passage, the speaker identifies the fixing power of the word, or as her earlier quotation from Deleuze and Guattari asserts, "The proper name is the instantaneous apprehension of a multiplicity" (1990, 41). The commentary on the ability of a word to transform the complexity and "multiplicity" of experience into something stable and fixed builds throughout the poem, becoming most pronounced in the above passage. After declaring that we enter "the word" rather than the real "forest," she then notes that in this word we enter a "trance" in which we see the land as pristine ("not a foot of land cleared"). The word "forest" is imbued with particularly pastoral undertones, which shape the way one experiences the word. For the speaker, those undertones take on a central role as she acknowledges the "trance" or "spell" that words bring with them ("The literature of savagism / under a spell of savagism") and that these words have the power to isolate one aspect of the physical world from the sometimes dark cultural, historical, and personal histories that lie within them ("Nature isolates the Adirondacks").

In a sense, then, this passage examines the distortive qualities of language that might best be understood in terms Timothy Morton establishes when he explains that "nature always slips out of reach in the very act of grasping it. At the very moment at which writing seems to be dissolving in the face of the compelling reality it is describing, writing overwhelms what it is depicting and makes it impossible to find anything behind its opaque texture" (2007, 19). Morton contends that the word or idea of "nature" brings with it limitations, so that naming something, as the speaker names the "forest," hides the complexity behind it. According to White, "Thorow" is an "interruption" of "the literary projects of savagism and the pastoral," an observation that aptly accounts for the speaker's reaction against the pastoral image of the uncleared forest (2006, 253). According to Morton, the speaker reacts against the pastoral by identifying the "trance" and "spell" that "isolates the Adirondacks" from their history and individual experiences of them. The commentary on language and nature in "Thorow" provides an important foundation for Howe's use of landscape throughout her poetics. Although the landscape appears to be an overt participant in the text, it is a troubled conception of place that makes its way into Howe's poetry. Rather than accepting language and landscape together, the poet identifies the ways in which they complicate and even impede each other. As she states in her interview with Keller, "pure feeling is connected to silence. Any mark or word would be a corruption of that infinite purpose or purposelessness" (Keller 1995, 7). The recognition of the enmeshment of language and the environment but also their contradictions shapes Howe's unnatural ecopoetics. In "Thorow" as in *The Midnight*, environment plays a significant role as the speaker struggles to contend with these limitations and locate a textual space that can adequately account for the multiplicity of physical environments in the limited forum of language.

## UNNATURAL ECOPOETICS IN *THE MIDNIGHT*

The role of environments in *The Midnight* is arguably less obvious than in some of Howe's other work. In fact, the book appears to be only minimally connected with concepts of space, as it leaves the reader thoroughly disoriented by its leaps between poetry and prose as well as shifts in content that range from inquiries into language to historical commentary. Traditional understandings of landscape or environment are not applicable to *The Midnight* because throughout the book material space is so deeply entwined with nonmaterial elements that shape it; however, if the concept of environment is broadened, the seemingly unnatural elements of Howe's poetry can be read for their environmental underpinnings. Through the lens of unnatural ecopoetics, the poem's disjointedness, coupled with its fascination with history, culture, memory, and language, can be viewed as attempts by the poet to adapt the multiple subjective elements that compose an individual's experience, including all of its diversions and inattentions, to text. For Howe, the page is a site or a space where the many elements of experience that are typically overlooked or underprivileged can be brought to the fore.

That the poet recognizes the many factors that influence perceptions of environment becomes apparent through the lens of unnatural ecopoetics, which specifically examines the naturalcultural elements of texts. An unnatural ecopoetic reading reveals that rather than excluding the individual perceiver from his or her context, Howe considers the ways in which environmental experiences are shaped by physical landscape, history, culture, and a variety of other factors. Throughout the book, some of these elements are emphasized more than others, but the speaker explicitly comments on her purpose in one of two prose sections, "Scare Quotes I," on her mother's move from Dublin to Boston. Here, the speaker affirms the power that text holds, ultimately claiming that "there were always three dimensions, visual, textual, and auditory. Waves of sound connected us by associational syllabic magic to an original but imaginary place existing somewhere across the ocean between the emphasis of sound and the emphasis of sense" (2003, 75). The speaker accepts the multiple "dimensions" that compose experience by pointing toward the "visual, textual, and auditory" and emphasizing the sensory aspect of it. Of similar importance, though, is her establishment of place—seemingly textual space—that is "imaginary" but also "existing somewhere" that is not entirely tangible. It is a space between "sound" and "sense," where neither one takes priority. This is arguably an outline for Howe's poetics. Her book similarly inhabits a middle space between pure form ("sound") and comprehension or logic ("sense"), always slipping back and forth between the two, just as it slips between poetry and prose, never fully settling on either side.

It is the poet's acknowledgment of middle spaces that leads to the unlikely environments of her poems, in which naturecultures are pulled to the fore. Although a pronounced focus on space appears foreign to Howe, she conceptualizes her work in environmental terms, stating that the naturalcultural fusion she recognizes through the "three dimensions" of experience are inherently spatial or environmental. In "Scare Quotes II," she writes that "environment itself is its own vast force. Peace, war, nuclear power, human population, immigration, famine, animal, fish, forest—lights go on and out in houses" (2003, 141). Recognizing that "environment" is composed not only of natural elements ("animal, fish, forest") but also of cultural ("immigration, famine"), political ("Peace, war, nuclear power"), and social ("human population") features, the speaker establishes a unique conception of environment that warrants the emphasis on naturecultures that an unnatural ecopoetic reading brings to the text. Approaching the book as a manifestation of the speaker's environmental sentiments reveals that Howe's poetics is not simply fragmented or disjointed but interested in expressing "the uncertain truth of fiction" (2003, 65). The book remains "uncertain" because it acknowledges multiplicity and subjectivity in perception and thus writing, which can allow for a "truth" but always only an "uncertain" one. In essence, then, Howe's poetics posits that all texts strive for "truth" but achieve only an "uncertain truth."

The speaker's acceptance of uncertainty and multiplicity is reflected in her formal choices, and as Marjorie Perloff puts it in *The Dance of the Intellect* (1985), "the articulation of an individual language is all but prevented by the official discourses that bombard the consciousness from all sides" (1985, 231). Like Hejinian, for Howe history and culture, or "official discourses," are always influencing the way experience is articulated. However, rather than attempting to overcome the mediation of material experiences, as Hejinian does, Howe chooses to acknowledge, embrace, and even highlight it. As such, *The Midnight* begins with a copy of a tissue paper interleaf from Robert Louis Stevenson's *The Master of Ballantrae*. Howe explains in the preface that "bookbinders placed [these sheets]…between frontispiece and title page in order to prevent illustration and text from rubbing together" (2003, n.p.). Immediately, the poet's commentary here harkens back to her own poetic form and ultimately her origins in visual arts, revealing that she is always aware of how words and reality mingle in her work. The opening image shows words behind a thick film, making it almost impossible to decipher the individual letters and often making the words illegible. By opening the book with this image and its accompanying commentary, the poet immediately foregrounds the inescapable influence of her book's historical predecessors on the project at hand. The placement of this murky image at the beginning implies that there is always such a historical and cultural film influencing and even obscuring a writer's new work. Perhaps even more importantly, she demonstrates that her work engages in much the same task as the tissue interleaf, which Perloff views as the central theme of the book in its illustration of "the contradiction between image and verbal caption" (2010, 107). Although destined to keep "illustration and text from rubbing together," both the interleaf and *The Midnight* imply that the two are always intertwined. As the interleaf's murky image shows, the text not only takes on but becomes an image.

Howe's acknowledgment of how multiple elements intermingle is an important facet of her poetry and one that facilitates her unnatural ecopoetics.

Rather than attempting to forget and separate history, culture, and other influences in order to "accurately" or objectively express the physical environment, the poet recognizes the role that history and culture play in experience and that the two are always rubbing together despite efforts to prevent it. By revealing from the beginning that her work is influenced by "official discourses" and accepting these as one of many influences on her experiences, Howe can more readily acknowledge how her own culture and personal history shape the poem, such as her mother and her Irish heritage, without abandoning her central interest in the gaps that occur when the real world is translated to language. From the perspective of unnatural ecopoetics, there are three major facets of the book that contribute to a naturalcultural rendering of experience: first, the influence of history and the problems with historical records; second, the power of personal emotions, memories, cultural influences, and the boundaries of one's perception; and third, explorations of both the promise and limitations of language and form. By breaking down the complex and often overlapping moves in the book into three distinct categories and then considering where those categories connect, we can begin to read *The Midnight* as a cohesive text and understand it as more than a purposely disjointed avant-garde poem; instead, we can see it as one that foregrounds through language and form the many influences, limitations, and oversights that shape real-world experiences.

Howe's naturalcultural conception of space is tied to the central motifs of the poem, one of the most prominent being history. Peter Quartermain claims that the poet's central purpose is to investigate the underserved figures in history.[3] Since much of Howe's writing, as Quartermain contends, retrieves historical figures who have been otherwise ignored, her work lends itself to historical readings. However, focusing solely on how the poet reaffirms the significance of history diminishes the important message throughout the book that history is largely subjective, a message the poet emphasizes by granting agency to written documents.

An unnatural ecopoetic approach reveals that the historical presences in her work shape the textual space of the poem. In "Bed Hangings I," the speaker considers the place and stability of history and its connection to language when she acknowledges the influence of writing on historical record, as in the following:

It is requested that those who
discover errors in this work
not mentioned in the ERRATA
should give information of them

to Mr. William L. Kingsley of
New Haven and if it seems
desirable they will be given to
the public together with other
facts and statistics ADDENDA
The great Disposer of events
is exchanging what was good
for what is better history that
is written will be accomplished

(2003, 38)

In this poem, the speaker emphasizes the lack of stability in historical records and documents their relationship to writing. Referencing William L. Kingsley, the longtime proprietor of the *New Englander and Yale Review* in the late nineteenth century, the poem comments on "errata" that might appear in writing. The speaker recounts how a reader might report an error and concludes that "if it seems / desirable" those errors will be corrected and "addenda" distributed "to / the public." In the process of correcting these errors, the editor, or as the speaker names him, "[t]he great Disposer of events," decides whether the corrected material "is better history." With this, the speaker suggests a subjectivity in what becomes documented history by revealing that the editor's discretion shapes it ("exchanging what was good / for what is better"). As such, the poem comments on the instability of history and its subjective documentation.

My approach highlights that writing makes the nonmaterial and material elements of experience tangible and active. Howe's speaker concludes with a bid toward writing's agential power; after acknowledging the instability of history, she declares that "history that / is written will be accomplished." The speaker claims that once "history" gets "written down," as in Kingsley's journal, it becomes tangible. Put another way, writing constitutes history. Following the previous line's comment on the unfixed nature of history, these final lines implicate language in the construction of worlds, suggesting that writing has real-world effects. In his discussion of "pure poetry" and history, Paul Naylor contends that Howe's writing is "temporal," "historical," and "linguistic, rather than naturalistic. In this sense, she participates in the tradition of pure poetry that seeks to create a world of words.... Yet the crucial difference between Howe and other pure poets... is that she does not attempt to seal this world off from the real world of historical fact but to make visible the holes in traditional historiography" (1999, 53). Unnatural ecopoetics reveals that the lack of stability in history is tied to the subjectivity in its selection and recording, a fact that

pulls the writer into the creation of both text and world while also recognizing that even seemingly stable elements like history or, to push further, physical experiences, are experienced subjectively.

The subjectivity of the writer is mirrored in the poem by the subjectivity
of the reader's encounter with the text. Still, here it is not Howe's reader's experience that demonstrates the subjective nature of experience, but the infusion
of historical and personal references into the text. In a discussion of her great
aunt, Louie Bennett, the poet notes that her aunt wrote in her copy of *The Irish
Song Book with Original Irish Airs*, "This book has a value for Louie Bennett
that it cannot have for any other human being. Therefore let no other human
being keep it in his possession" (2003, 59). The words are typed out below a
photograph of the page itself, on which Bennett's words are visible. For her
aunt, the book's power comes from her individual reading of it or, alternatively,
her encounter with the physical book as an object to be experienced subjectively rather than something fixed and objective. But the speaker questions
whether blindly obeying nondisturbance is the best way to preserve history.
She goes on to ask:

> How can the same volume contain so many different incompatible
> intrinsic relations? The Bennetts and Mannings are Irish and not Irish
> so we haven't the secret of our first ancestral parents. Names are only
> a map we use for navigating. Disobeying Aunt Louie's predatory with-
> drawal, or preservative denial, I recently secured the spine of her *Irish
> Song Book* with duct tape. Damage control—its cover was broken. So
> your edict flashes daggers—so what. (2003, 59)

In this section, the text oscillates between prose commentary and photography,
fusing multiple forms while simultaneously explaining how and why one must
embrace new forms to express and preserve history. Perloff points out that the
progression of this section, typical of Howe's work, is from clear descriptive
language toward elliptical contemplation (2010, 102). After first acknowledging that "the same volume" can be read differently and even incompatibly, the
speaker admits her willingness to disobey her aunt's "predatory withdrawal"
that asks others to leave her copy of the book untouched and instead does
"damage control" by taping the book's broken spine. The instability that she
identifies in the book, like the instability of historical record identified in the
poem on Kingsley, is tied to language, as she implies in saying that "names are
only a map we use for navigating." As in the previous passage, language becomes unfixed and flexible to the moment. Naylor's understanding of history's
role in the book contextualizes this moment; he contends that "the events in

history are not, despite appearances, woven into a seamless, hypotactic narrative; information has been, intentionally and unintentionally, left out. Without that information, without the normal hypotactic connections between elements within the narrative, we become, as Howe puts it in another poem, 'Lost in language,' although 'we are language'" (1999, 61). Ultimately, the speaker's willingness to challenge the historical record of her aunt and risk altering the record in the process is grounded in the previous section's questioning of the stability of history. As she acknowledges the subjectivity and instability of historical record, she begins to challenge the traditional methods of preserving history, a challenge that shapes her poetic form.

The speaker's recognition that the historical record requires new forms of expression to remain relevant to the present moment is the sentiment that orients the book toward an unnatural ecopoetic reading. Recognizing that history plays a role in how individuals experience texts and worlds while also realizing the flexibility or subjectivity in historical record, the speaker experiments with new forms that emerge from her own experience of history. In "Scare Quotes I," she writes that

> The relational space is the thing that's alive with something from somewhere else. Jonathan Edwards was a paper saver. He kept old bills and shopping lists, then copied out his sermons on the verso sides and stitched them into handmade notebooks. When he was in his twenties, Emerson cut his dead minister father's sermons in manuscript out of their bindings, then used the bindings to hold his own writing. He mutilated another of Emerson senior's notebooks in order to use the blank pages. Stubs of torn off paper show sound bites. (2003, 58)

The naturalcultural foundations of the text are clearly expressed in this passage, as the speaker explicitly comments on the power of fusion. Emerging from her interrogation of history, the speaker contends that "space" becomes "alive" when it is fused "with something from somewhere else." Here, she grounds this fusion in history by recounting the cutting, splicing, and synthesis in the work of Edwards and Emerson. Both writers destruct original texts and rearrange or rework them for new purposes, practicing a type of recycling that is reminiscent of Howe's own formal structure. The influence of history is mingled with personal influences and family history later in the book when the speaker states, "often you must turn Uncle John's books around and upside down to read the clippings and other insertions pasted and carefully folded inside" (2003, 143). Harkening back to the poet's own formal experimentation, this passage's reference to her "Uncle John" reveals a familial connection.

On the one hand, these passages demonstrate that her form is rooted in historical methods and family history. On the other hand, her foregrounding of the forces that shape her text allows the reader to identify those influences and better understand how, when, and where those forces are at work in the book.

Foregrounding the book's textuality and influences is a central concern in unnatural ecopoetics and, as the prose and poetry sections reveal, to the poet. In an earlier poetry section, she similarly comments on how the fusion of history, text, language, and here economics creates a textual space in which all of these influences are at the fore; but despite their disclosure, a viable space still emerges. The poem reads:

> Surviving fragment of
> New England original
> bed hanging handsome
> cambleteen red curtain
> (1746) "a sort of fine
> worsted cambels" Camlet
> Imitation camlet scrap
> To describe Camlet I will
> Look into Chambers and
> Postlethwayt

(2003, 15)

The poem begins with the "bed hanging" that inspires the section's title. The "[s]urviving fragment," the speaker explains, was crafted in 1746 out of "Camlet / Imitation camlet scrap." The speaker's focus on the material of the curtain is related to the interest in fusion that becomes apparent later in the text. In this poem, the camlet, a type of fabric woven out of camel hair or angora wool, is seen as "imitation," a copy of the authentic material. Since the poem considers the bed hanging that dominates this section of the book, the identification of it as "imitation" is particularly important. Recognizing that the material is only a copy calls into question the authenticity of the section titled "Bed Hangings I." As the curtain is composed of copied material, so too is the section, which, like the fabric, weaves together copied material from history, culture, memory, and language. The poem concludes by overtly acknowledging the naturalcultural fusions it embraces by turning toward something contemporaneous to the bed hanging but otherwise unrelated to the scene—economics—to describe the physical material of the curtains. In turning to "Chambers and Postlethwayt" to "describe" the "Camlet," the speaker incorporates economics and history into her understanding of the physical object and its historical role. Postlethwayt was "one of the leading economists before Adam Smith.... His writings helped American revolutionaries justify attacks on Britain's 'unfair taxes,' and laid foundations for chambers of commerce" (Bennett 2011, 187). Since cutting and splicing make "space" come "alive," the poet turns to economic theory contemporaneous to the bed hanging to describe the physical manifestation of history—the remnants of the curtain—making the present fragments of the object in its current place and its history come to life for the reader. In this way, the poem demonstrates how multiple elements compose a particular experience, pulling the historical, textual, personal, material, and economic into a single space.

While many Howe critics argue that history is at the heart of the poet's work, a closer examination of the historical presences in the book through the lens of unnatural ecopoetics reveals that history is employed as only one of many elements that constitute an experience. The speaker engages with history subjectively, recognizing its instability and that it benefits from new methods of preservation. Historical data is not best preserved by leaving it untouched and pristine, but through new methods of expressing it in which historical records are contextualized by the contemporary moment. To be sure, history is important or even vital in Howe's work, but it is employed with other elements of experience that fuse together to form a single naturalcultural environment on the page. *The Midnight* engages with naturecultures not only by employing history but also by considering the personal connections to that history that shape the writer. Throughout the book, including some of the sections previously discussed, the poet's family history is fused with historical data, making public history and personal history indistinguishable.

Returning, for instance, to the copy of the interleaf from *The Master of Ballantrae* that opens *The Midnight*, Howe's references to historical moments are tied to her own personal histories. The inclusion of the tissue paper interleaf demonstrates a clear interest in visual arts, poetic form, collage, and historical record, and is linked to a specific part of the poet's personal life. In "Scare Quotes I," she informs us that "several years ago I inherited John Manning's heavily marked up copy of Robert Louis Stevenson's *The Master of Ballantrae: A Winter's Tale*" (2003, 53). As the speaker reveals that the poet's history is tied up in the formal and historical elements of the text, the influence of her own personal history on the poem becomes apparent. Perloff outlines the multiple directions of the book when she explains how "*The Midnight* points both *outside* the text to the countless memoirs, biographies, and gossip about this or that Irish writer, actor, or relative who had anything to do with the poet's maternal background, and *inside* its covers to the diverse and contradictory clues that are woven together to create the book's 'factual telepathy'" (2010, 106). In this way, the reproduced interleaf conveys a message similar to the one of the Louie Bennett passage previously discussed, as it suggests that everything is imbued with personal and family history, influences that shape and even create meaning. For the speaker, the "value" in Louie Bennett's book lay in her material copy, just as the inclusion of the interleaf from Stevenson's book is explained by its personal significance. The poet chose to include a piece that is not only historical but has profound personal ties. In this way, her engagement with public and personal history is integrated because each shapes the other.

The poet's personal connections to the historical data referenced in the text shape her formal choices. While her radical experimentation might appear to relate to language poetry, as other scholars have contended, a close reading of *The Midnight* reveals that her form is more readily linked to her understanding of how these various ways of experiencing the world—historically, culturally, personally, and materially—are fused. Later in "Scare Quotes I," the speaker comments on these connections when she reflects on the lives of the books that enter the text:

> My mother's close relations treated their books as transitional objects (judging by a few survivors remaining in my possession) to be held, loved, carried around, meddled with, abandoned, sometimes mutilated. They contain dedications, private messages, marginal annotations, hints, snapshots, press cuttings, warnings—scissor work. Some volumes have been shared as scripts for family theatricals. When something in the world is cross-identified, it just is. *They* have made this relation by gathering—airs, reveries, threads, mythologies, nets, oilskins, briars and branches, wishes and needs, intact—into a sort of tent. This is a space children used to play in. (2003, 60)

In a moment of self-reflexive commentary, the speaker clearly connects the personal history of the texts with their role within the book. Commenting that her family members viewed their books as things "to be held, loved, carried around, meddled with, abandoned, sometimes mutilated," and included within them extratextual data ("dedications, private messages, marginal annotations, hints, snapshots, press cuttings, warnings—scissor work"), the speaker emphasizes the materiality of the books as objects. An object-oriented ontology might help to elucidate this scene by emphasizing the thingness of the books and their independent actions on individuals as well as on the text. In emphasizing "the it as actant," as Jane Bennett proposes, readers could view the books as acting on her family members and, later, acting on the shape of Howe's own project

(2010, 3). Her family members integrated the books into their lives, carrying them with them, infusing them with their daily experiences, and ultimately recreating them through contextual and material alterations. As a result, the books that the speaker references throughout *The Midnight* are not simply copies of the original texts, but objects infused with a great deal of personal history that alters the overall meaning of Howe's project and, to some extent, things with their own agential power. For Howe, in the case of *Ballantrae*, for instance, it is not the book's content that is significant, but its expression of the life that it lived in her family. The inclusion of the book, then, infuses public history into the text while also bringing with it a wealth of personal connections and memories for the poet. Writing that "when something in the world is cross-identified, it just is," the speaker articulates a naturalcultural sentiment, in which the textual space of the book is infused with physical movement ("carried around"), external influences ("private messages," "press cuttings"), and individual emotions ("loved," "abandoned"). Howe's unnatural ecopoetics emerges, then, through her fusion of these various spaces into the text.

In this passage, the books that the poet references are clearly revealed as both naturalcultural and spatial, illuminating the methodology behind her ecopoetics and exemplifying her conception of space. Rachel Back points out that the poet's environments are complicated by historical and personal significance, contending that

> place is, for Howe, a site of specific voices that need to be listened to—voices of literal territories (that is, New York State's Lake George, Dublin's the Liberties) that she traverses, inhabits, examines, and that at all times infiltrate and influence the form and content of her work. Place is also a reflection of the work's integrity, as expressed in her poetry's exclusive preoccupation with landscapes to which she feels she in some way belongs, is connected to, and created by: poetry is, for Howe, an act of self-involvement and self-revelation. (2002, 8)

Pushing Back's argument even further, I would say that place in Howe's work is composed of multiple elements, and often multiple genres and forms, that express the poet's "self-involvement and self-revelation." In the passage, the speaker states that the books gain significance by being "cross-identified," a connection that results from their accumulation of "airs, reveries, threads, mythologies, nets, oilskins, briars and branches, wishes and needs." Here, the nonmaterial or subjective elements of experience and the material aspects of space that shape the books are fused "into a sort of tent" or single structure. The physical ("nets," "briars and branches"), the historical ("mythologies"), and the personal ("airs, reveries," "wishes and needs") are combined into a single structure, a fusion that facilitates being ("it just is"). Now "cross-identified," the books come into being and become textual spaces tangible enough for children to play in. The connection between the various elements of the text and physical space in this passage create what the poet calls "a document universe," or a world composed of words and the various elements that constitute them (2003, 61).

The way Howe explains textual space in this passage is powerfully supported by the formal elements of the book—namely her inclusion of various elements from family, textual, and public history. Aside from discussions and descriptions of these elements, the poet includes photographs of various objects, ranging from portraits and paintings to book pages and postage stamps. The inclusion of these objects is puzzling largely for their highly unconventional placement within the poetic context but also because many of them depict objects or scenes that are already described in the text. In *Visual Culture*, Margaret Dikovitskaya observes that "art plays the role of literature despite a fundamental difference between, on the one hand, visual imaging and picturing and, on the other, linguistic expression: Language is based on a system (syntax, grammar, phonology) that can be scientifically described whereas pictures cannot" (2005, 56). By including both the image and textual discussion of its content, the poet calls into question the ability of the word to depict the world through what Dikovitskaya describes as language's system. Perloff argues that "the found text and illustration measure the absurdity of Howe's situation more fully than could any direct narrative account" (2010, 121). In other words, Perloff contends that the fusion of various elements throughout the book, including the visual, give a truer account of the lived moment than words alone can. The inclusion of images throughout the text, then, serves as a reminder of the limitations of language.

Language's limitations are prominent throughout *The Midnight*. Although these moments are often overlooked in favor of references to public and family history, Howe shows a profound interest in the ability and failure of language to express real-world experience. The poet foregrounds language's limitations both through the poem's content and the inclusion of photographs that are not limited by language's system or rules. The contrast that the photographs raise between the clear expression of visual arts and the restrictions of language is articulated by the speaker immediately after her discussion of her family's relationship with books. She writes, "Words sounding as seen the same moment on paper will always serve as the closest I can come to cross-identification vis-à-vis counterparts in a document universe" (2003, 61). After this, the text breaks for a line that includes all the letters of the alphabet. In this moment, the speaker states that "the closest" she can come to "cross-identification," or being, is based on words "sounding as seen the same moment," which implies a disjunction between the visual and the written. In a similar comment made during the interview with Keller, the poet comments on the connection between the lived or seen experience and the written version of it: "You're hearing something you see. And there's the mystery of the eye-hand connection: when it's your work, it's your hand writing. Your hand is receiving orders from somewhere. Yes, it could be your brain, your superego giving orders; on the other hand, they *are* orders" (quoted in Keller 1995, 33; emphasis in original). Here, Howe reveals that she views writing as mediated by other forces, whether it be the brain or otherwise. The physical experience or sensation is never the same when translated to language. For the poet, language is limited to the alphabet, a system that constrains its ability to express the world. However, by foregrounding language's limitations as she does in *The Midnight*, the poet conveys a natural-cultural experience by supplementing her text with visual images. Providing multiple perspectives, visual and written, on the same object, person, or scene, the poem achieves a sort of multi-angle telling that acknowledges and accepts the limitations of language.

The unnatural ecopoetics of *The Midnight* hinges on the poet's attempt to acknowledge and navigate the gap between world and word, a quest that is powerfully expressed throughout the book through an investigation into language's limitations. In the preface, the speaker comments: "Although a sign is understood to be consubstantial with the thing or being it represents, word and picture are essentially rivals" (2003, n.p.). In many ways, these lines outline Howe's project. Considering how to best make use of language and form to express a naturalcultural experience, she explores what language can and cannot accomplish. In "Scare Quotes I," Howe writes:

> If at the heart of language lies what language can't express, can it be false to say that the golden mountain which exists exists? O light and dark vowels with your transconsistent hissing and hushing I know you curtain I sense delusion. Fortunately we can capture for our world some soft object, a fuzzy conditional, a cot cover, an ode, a couplet, a line, a lucky stone—to carry around when camping. (2003, 70)

The speaker contends that "the heart of language" is inexpressible, implying that the impetus for writing is something beyond language. Or as Peter Quartermain artfully explains, "while the text longs for resolution, it insistently demands that its disorder not be dissipated in mere definition" (1992, 192). The inexpressibility or lack of clear definitions is central to the text's purpose. The inexpressible "heart of language" is an experience that is comprehensible in the physical world but not translatable to words. Pointing toward the rules that limit language ("vowels"), she suggests that even in its vagueness ("light and dark vowels with your transconsistent hissing and hushing") language attempts to express the lived experience, deluding the reader into believing it does so accurately ("I know you curtain I sense delusion"). Foregrounding the limitations of language, she observes that despite its inaccuracy to the physical world, language holds the power to express some version of it ("a fuzzy conditional"). In other words, the speaker acknowledges that while "language can't express" the "golden mountain," it can capture details or moments in that lived experience. It is, then, in an "object" or a "fuzzy" representation of the world that language operates for Howe. Still, despite its inaccuracy, the power of language is the portability ("to carry around when camping") of ideas that it facilitates. Only through language can ideas move from place to place and person to person. In this sense, language, while flawed and limited, is the only available tool to transport complex ideas, especially "fuzzy" but artistic messages ("an ode, a couplet, a line") from one person to another.

Although Howe's foregrounding of the limitations of language is most articulate in the prose sections of the book, these moments are also evident in the poetry sections of the book. An early poem in the book reads:

> Go too—my savage pattern
> on surface material the line
> in ink if you have curtains
> and a New English Dictionary
> there is nothing to justify a
> claim for linen except a late
> quotation knap warp is flax
> Fathom we without cannot

> (2003, 8)

The speaker identifies her poem as a "savage pattern" that appears in "the line." Recognizing the constructedness of her own writing as reliant on "a New English Dictionary," paper or "linen," and a stolen "quotation," Howe foregrounds the problems that exist with traditional poetry. To break away from such "savage pattern[s]," she alters the language itself. As the speaker recognizes these issues, the language breaks down into a jumbled version of the original ("Fathom we without cannot"), making it difficult, if not impossible, for the reader to decipher the literal meaning of the line. The breakdown of language in this poem reflects the limited reach of language in expressing the lived experience behind it. Quartermain emphasizes the poet's commentary on language as pushing against the content of the text when he contends that "Howe's writing arises from a series of tensions, between the more-or-less explicit themes and subject matter of the work, and the unstated verbal and schematic activity of the poem" (1992, 183). The "explicit themes" of her work, apparent both in the poem and the prose passage previously discussed, although seemingly focused on history and personal connections, are fundamentally tied to language.

In many ways, Howe's commentary on language is mimicked by her formal choices throughout the book. Oscillating between poetry and prose while integrating personal reflections, photographs, and historical data, the book represents a truly unique poetic form in which the poet attempts to preserve the disjunction of lived experience on the page. As such, Howe's critique of language is coupled with a distinct concern for how the complexity and simultaneity of experience is deflated in text, both linguistically and formally. One of the book's early poems reads:

> Counterforce brings me wild hope
> non-connection is itself distinct
> connection numerous surviving
> fair trees wrought with a needle
> the merest decorative suggestion
> in what appears to be sheer white
> muslin a tree fair hunted Daphne
> Thinking is willing you are wild
> to the weave not to material itself

(2003, 17)

Out of context, this poem has little significance. In fact, its lack of punctuation and seemingly nonsensical utterances make it initially incomprehensible. Considering the poet's interest in language, however, this poem connects important conversations about language in the prose sections with the significantly denser poetry sections. As the speaker states here, disjointedness does not necessarily bring incomprehensibility or uselessness; rather, acknowledging and preserving the complexity and variety of lived experience creates a truer representation of reality than one that attempts to fill those gaps. The speaker states that "non-connection is itself distinct / connection," highlighting the importance of acknowledging such gaps. It is, in fact, when connection is imposed on the lived experience that problems arise. Claiming that "trees wrought with a needle," or tied together neatly but unnaturally by the human observer, are altered by "the merest decorative suggestion" in their otherwise pure existence ("sheer white / muslin"), the speaker reveals that to force connection actually creates disconnection. She concludes by claiming that "Thinking" demands that one allow lived experience to maintain its nonconnection or disjointedness ("wild / to the weave") even as one acknowledges and values such lived experience ("not to material itself").

For Howe, history, personal remembrances, language, physical experience, and form are tied up in the text. Throughout both the poetry and prose sections of the book, she foregrounds the limitations of language while simultaneously working to create a textual space that can accommodate the various naturalcultural elements of experience. In essence, the book acts much like the interleaf of *The Master of Ballantrae*. As the speaker says, "this thinnest blank sheet should be mute but it's noisily nondescript. The interleaf shelters the frontispiece though it's flimsy and somewhat slippery" (2003, 57). The interleaf "shelters" the book itself, the actual object, but it is "noisily nondescript" because it is "flimsy" and "slippery." In this way, the interleaf acts much as language does, appearing as a murky but untrue expression of the frontispiece but never actually standing in for the original. For Howe, this is the position of language. It acts as a murky expression of lived experience, always trying to stand in for the real-world original but remaining a blurred, unclear copy. Just as we acknowledge the interleaf as not standing in for the original frontispiece, we must recognize that words cannot stand in for lived experience. Considering her poetry through the lens of unnatural ecopoetics, it is clear that Howe's work posits that we must accept that lived experience can never fully be expressed on the page but only approached through text and form. In this way, the book is profoundly engaged with unnatural ecopoetics. In examining the limitations of language and the possibilities of form, *The Midnight* is well suited to an unnatural ecopoetic reading as it considers how to express the simultaneity and multiplicity of experience while acknowledging and accepting the limitations of its own medium.

## CONCLUSION

To discuss Howe from the perspective of ecopoetics initially can seem unjustified. Given the traditional images of nature highly disembodied by formal and linguistic play and considering the highly disorienting form of her text, Howe's work seems to run counter to most conceptions of environment. However, Howe is uniquely engaged with the variety, multiplicity, and simultaneity of lived experience, recognizing that no one element shapes it alone, but rather that experience is tied to many subjective elements at once. The textual space of the book is made up of these various facets, coming together to create a naturalcultural space. In one of the most profound moments in the book, the speaker writes that *The Midnight* is "assembling materials for a recurrent return somewhere. Familiar sound textures, deliverances, vagabond quotations, preservations, wilderness shrubs, little resuscitated patterns. Historical or miraculous. Thousands of correlations have to be sliced and spliced" (2003, 85). It is this variety of components that makes Howe's textual space so authentic to lived experience because the poet acknowledges the text's constructedness and foregrounds the variety of material and nonmaterial elements that shape it. She recognizes that her pages are not the same as lived experience but uses novel forms and a variety of elements to attempt to express on the page the multiple influences that shape experience. To do so, Howe employs radical experimentation, collage, visual arts, and linguistic play to not only acknowledge but foreground language's limitations and explore the possibilities of such open forms.

Despite the lack of traditional environments in Howe's work, her engagement with naturalcultural spaces and her infusion of them into her texts exemplifies the unnatural ecopoetic sentiments in *The Midnight*. For Howe, the foregrounded textual spaces that she creates must account for the many histories, personal memories, emotional entanglements, formal nuances, and physical realities of lived experience while also acknowledging that text can never equal the world. However, in *The Midnight* text does not need to equal the lived experience to be effective. The book accepts, as its speaker states, that the "environment itself is its own vast force," composed of a variety of naturalcultural elements, and the text, too, is a force (2003, 141). A textual space has the power to create what Howe terms "counterparts in a document universe," which reveal the many influences that shape material experience (2003, 61). Indeed, the book's power emerges because "the story inside its covers has another conscious life" (2003, 61). By granting Howe's text autonomy, readers discover that the textual space of *The Midnight* is more than just a failed copy or mimic of the lived world but a world in itself.

### NOTES

1. As I will discuss in the coming pages, Howe's poem "Thorow" has received some critical attention for its connection to landscape, and Scott Knickerbocker's 2012 book, *Ecopoetics: The Language of Nature, the Nature of Language*, briefly discusses Howe's *Articulation of Sound Forms in Time* in its conclusion.

2. In Keller's interview with her, Howe specifically discusses why she objects to being identified as a language poet (1995, 19–20). Allen identifies her as a language poet, but others, like Linda Reinfeld, contend that critics should be cautious about associating Howe with her contemporary poets.

3. In *Disjunctive Poetics: From Gertrude Stein and Louis Zukofsky to Susan Howe*, Peter Quartermain observes that "Howe is, more than any American writer I can think of except perhaps Melville or Henry Adams, burdened by history: The burden, of retrieving from erasure and marginality those (women) who have been written out, without (as Howe puts it in her prose introduction to 'Thorow') appropriating primal indeterminacy, is compounded by the drift of the primal toward the immediate, toward the abolition of history (and hence of language) altogether" (1992, 194).

# [ 4 ]

## The Agency of Found Text
## in Kenneth Goldsmith's
### *Seven American Deaths and Disasters*

*With the rise of the Web, writing has met its photography.*
*By that, I mean writing has encountered a situation similar*
*to what happened to painting with the invention of photography,*
*a technology so much better at replicating reality that,*
*in order to survive, painting had to alter its course radically.*

—KENNETH GOLDSMITH, *Uncreative Writing*

KENNETH GOLDSMITH's *Seven American Deaths and Disasters* (2013) is a found conceptual poem that transcribes radio and television reports of a number of national deaths and disasters. The book is "fascinated with rendering the mundane in language" (2013, 169). In found poems like Goldsmith's, language is extracted directly from human representations of the lived experience— cultural, digital, natural, and political. As Goldsmith transcribes reports from real-world events, he expresses those moments without further translating them through the poet's own language; instead he takes a variety of cultural artifacts and puts them together on paper in order to illustrate the complex narratives that constructed that moment. Goldsmith, who rose to fame in 2015 for con- troversially applying the same principles of transcription to Michael Brown's autopsy report, does not attempt to overcome the limitations of human per- ception by expressing a pseudo-authentic experience, but rather foregrounds, to an even greater degree than Susan Howe, the inevitably murky filter through which human beings are destined to view the world. Recent developments in new materialism, which posit that the human is deeply enmeshed within his or her surroundings and ultimately one with them, reveal that despite the lack of traditional images of "nature" in *Seven American Deaths and Disasters* and its radical enmeshment in pop culture, Goldsmith's book is highly ecopoetic in its attempts to convey the material and nonmaterial elements that compose real-world experiences and demonstrates their agential power through their noticeable influences on experience.

Although in the past Goldsmith would not have been read as an ecopoet, unnatural ecopoetics lends itself to analyzing his work. As ecopoetics moves beyond traditional ideas of nature and environmental experience toward a more multifaceted approach to the various divergent and sometimes unconnected elements that compose a lived moment, it becomes increasingly tied to the tenets of conceptual writing (and ultimately conceptual art) that investigate not only what is experienced but also how such experience is shaped. A full understanding of the connections between ecopoetics and conceptual writing, however, requires some familiarity with the theories and history behind conceptual movements. The drive toward conceptual or appropriative art, of course, begins with Marcel Duchamp's famous ready-made pieces, ranging from the widely known urinal to a typewriter cover unprecedentedly reconceptualized for the art space. Duchamp revolutionized the art world by taking found everyday objects like the urinal and, as Craig Dworkin puts it in "The Fate of Echo," redeploying them in the context of the gallery, where they could be conceived of as art (2011, xxv). The conceptual movement propels the art world toward a breaking down of the boundaries of art and life. Art is no longer an object removed from everyday life, but something extracted from it. Dworkin explains that this conceptual art works because "the simple act of reframing seemed to refresh one's view of even familiar works, which appear significantly different by virtue of their new context" (2011, xxiv). Duchamp's recontextualization of the urinal forever changed the way individuals interpret the everyday object and understand the concept of art. When the familiar is pulled into a new space, the material opens new avenues for inquiry and investigation.

As Darren Hudson Hick puts it in "Forgery and Appropriation in Art," after Duchamp, artists like Andy Warhol and Roy Lichtenstein pushed the boundaries of appropriation art even further by drawing images from pop culture, but the movement reached its climax with artist Sherrie Levine's exhibition of photographs of photographs by another artist (2010, 1052). As appropriation art develops, then, it moves from the recontextualization of everyday objects to what ultimately appears to be a kind of forgery when it reappropriates other works of art. Hick explains that "although the term 'appropriation art' has been used to refer to the appropriation of ideas, to cultural borrowing, and the collage and assemblage works of Dadaists and pop artists, the term has come to be more closely associated with the work of Levine and others who reproduce pre-existing works outright" (2010, 1052). Appropriation art is now viewed primarily as an act of theft or forgery. Unlike Duchamp's recontextualization of the everyday object, these later appropriation pieces seek to reframe art itself, thus drawing attention to its original meaning, goals, and place while also giving it a new purpose.

This Levine-inspired appropriation art is arguably tied to the unique developments and challenges of new generations. In 1980, when Levine broke new ground, the world was quite different from that of Duchamp: beginning to engage more and more with emerging technologies and facing an increasingly uncertain political future, the 1980s were radically different from the serene prewar environment of the 1910s. Furthermore, these developments have continued far beyond Levine's 1980 exhibition. The twenty-first century brings different challenges than those faced by earlier artists, yet the theory of appropriation art is still relevant to contemporary theory and continues to develop in unlikely ways. Today, as Goldsmith's philosophy demonstrates, appropriation art has expanded beyond the visual arts world and into poetry. Contemporary poets have taken Levine's ideas to the next level, not only recontextualizing photographs but also plagiarizing without any frame whatsoever to foreground the appropriation. This new conceptual poetry, or even more specifically, appropriation poetry, pulls the everyday into the poetic space to encourage a new perspective on it.

To some degree, the evolution of appropriation art and writing stems from the growing Western investment in technology that permeates everyday life and alters the way we perceive and interact with the world. In the twenty-first century, the lived environmental experience is mediated, shaped, or dictated by virtual data ranging from mapping software, to digital game-space, to advanced visual conferencing, to hyper-portable digital music devices. These technological advancements alter the ways in which individuals experience the world, releasing massive numbers of possible scenarios and allowing each person an entirely subjective encounter with the same place and time. The revolution of experience brought on by the digital age demands new types of art and novel methods of expressing the world. In her book on appropriation writing, *Unoriginal Genius: Poetry by Other Means in the New Century*, Marjorie Perloff highlights the challenge that the digital age presents for literature. She observes that the contemporary writer is faced with "an environment of hyper-information, an environment, moreover, where we are all authors" (2010, xi). Perloff's statement illustrates two new concerns for the literary world. The first is that writing is no longer reserved for the elite few, no longer rare, and no longer locked away from the general population in a complex web of publishing houses and editors. Today, writing is produced at a rapid and constant rate;

the age of "hyperinformation" brings with it an age of hypertext. The second implication of Perloff's statement is that writing can be altered, developed, changed, and moved at any given moment. Unlike in the past, words are not fixed on a page but available on a screen for the average user to copy, paste, plagiarize, alter, or delete.

Goldsmith, who is generally considered the founder of conceptual poetry, argues that developments in technology, which change the role of the writer and simultaneously make words reproduce exponentially, demand a new approach to writing. Yet, critics of conceptual writing contend that the movement is not a response to the changing reality of contemporary culture but simply a misguided attempt to debunk poetry. Calvin Bedient, for instance, in "Against Conceptualism: Defending the Poetry of Affect," observes that conceptual art emerges as an attempt to challenge the capitalist threads running through the art world and proclaims that "current conceptual writers, though descendants of the conceptual artists, defy only the institution of poetry, which, no doubt fortunately, seldom dirties its hands with big money.... Its target is the supposed naïveté of literature that aspires to be original, hence writing that is likely to be affectual" (2013, 74). Bedient rightly points out that conceptual writing evolves from conceptual art and that it does not necessarily seek affect. However, Bedient does not acknowledge the ways in which the shift toward conceptual appropriation poetry is, unlike the conceptual art of Duchamp, Warhol, and Levine, the product of a contemporary world in which technology has made words more prevalent and more formative in everyday life. In Motoko Rich's article on the changes in reading styles in the twenty-first century, Dr. Rand J. Spiro points out that today's young people do not expect reading material to "go in a line...[and] [t]hat's a good thing because the world doesn't go in a line, and the world isn't organized into separate compartments or chapters" (quoted in Rich 2008, par. 13). Spiro's point is that today's youth have adapted to a new type of reading, one that is present in the forms of entertainment like online networking, chatting, and Web browsing, with which they engage for hours on end each day. The seemingly wasted time spent on the Internet, though, is time spent encountering language and ultimately, as Spiro concludes, is reading. The Internet has simply changed what it means to read or write and how individuals read or write. Bedient's article ignores that shift. As reading and writing evolve alongside technology, so too must poetry change if it is to engage with the concerns of contemporary culture.

Perloff contends that the adaptation to a changing cultural environment is most apparent in contemporary appropriation methods. In praise of conceptual poetry, she contends that this style of writing engages more with larger debates than many earlier forms. She argues that in the twenty-first century, poetics is moving away from language poetry's methods of resistance and toward "dialogue," a shift that she views as dependent on conversations with other texts and engaging with larger, more public exchanges. She attributes this specifically to a shifting poetic landscape in which "*Inventio* is giving way to appropriation, elaborate constraint, visual and sound composition, and reliance on intertextuality. Thus we are witnessing a new poetry, more conceptual than directly expressive" (Perloff 2010, 11). For Perloff, contemporary poetry increasingly hinges on the process of "appropriation." No longer invested in originality or "invention" or even "expression," some contemporary poets are choosing to create by recycling or simply transplanting the work of others. The movement toward appropriation is evident in my discussion of Susan Howe's placement of found text and images in chapter 3 and is evident in the work of poets like Walter Benjamin, Charles Bernstein, Charles Reznikoff, Robert Fitterman, Anne Carson, and Vanessa Place.[1]

Directly contradicting Bedient's harsh critique of conceptual poetry, Reznikoff's midcentury adaptation of court documents into his epic poem *Testimony* (1978) reveals the power of appropriation to convey complex emotions and influence conceptions of a particular place and time. His work opens the door to literary appropriation that becomes more feasible in the recent technological age. Unlike Reznikoff's edited court-documents-turned-poetry, Place's *Tragodia 1: Statement of Facts* (2011), which Dworkin and Goldsmith view as a reappropriation of Reznikoff's work, is a noninterventionist appropriation of the briefs the poet wrote in her work as a lawyer (Dworkin and Goldsmith 2011, 489). Leaving the documents unedited, aside from anonymizing them for privacy, Place's work redeploys Reznikoff's concept for the copy-and-paste generation of the twenty-first century. The appropriation in Place's work appears to be simple copying and entirely unoriginal. Yet, in recontextualizing the words, the poet constructs a complex commentary on "issues of labor, value, surplus, expenditure, context, recontext: uncompromising realism" (Dworkin and Goldsmith 2011, 489). What initially appears to be simple plagiarism is able to comment on complex issues in what is for her a more insightful and authentic manner than a highly formulated, mediated, and diluted formal text. In this approach, not only the physical events themselves and the emotional responses to them but also the cultural dialogue that shapes them are foregrounded and revealed to the reader.

The conceptual nature of this poetry does not remove it from the reality of everyday life. In fact, I contend that its appropriation ties this work more closely to the realities of real-world experiences than other poetic modes that claim to present authentic expressions of lived moments. The appropriated work, rather, foregrounds its limitations within language and begins by accepting and embracing those limitations. Joseph Kosuth's *Purloined: A Novel* (2000),[2] for instance, while composed of appropriated materials, employs a methodology that is deeply engrained with the artistic, cultural, historical, and political spaces that compose lived moments. The author photocopies pages from a variety of novels, compiling them to form a single novel. Although the words are plagiarized, the book's concept is entirely new and uniquely expressive of the culture in which the appropriated novels appeared, and the book comments on the culture in which the book is composed. In *Notes on Conceptualisms*, Vanessa Place and Robert Fitterman write that "allegorical writing (particularly in the form of appropriated conceptual writing) does not aim to critique the culture industry from afar, but to mirror it directly. To do so, it uses the materials of the culture industry directly" (2009, 20). Although Place and Fitterman view appropriation as a critique, which is perhaps more rooted in some forms of appropriation than it is in others,[3] they helpfully point to the ways in which appropriation mirrors culture. By drawing the language of particular cultural artifacts into a new space, a book like Kosuth's mirrors that culture, ultimately allowing the reader to view it in a new light and with new expectations. This appropriated work, then, reveals the culture from which it draws by foregrounding the language in which the work was originally expressed, ultimately demanding critical examination of the words as words, and often contrasting that language with alternate expressions of the same place, time, or culture.

With the shift toward appropriation, as Kenneth Goldsmith proclaims in *Uncreative Writing*, it becomes clear that in the twenty-first century, "*context is the new content*" (2011, 3; emphasis in original). These new poets are responding not just to the proliferation of the Internet, but also to the increased investment in all things digital throughout the past decade. In "Recycling Recycling or plus ça change...," Marilyn Randall rightly identifies shifting poetic landscapes as distinctly tied to cultural revolutions, arguing that "the concept of *intertextuality* (followed closely by *bricolage, appropriation*, and *recycling*)... [fulfill] a theoretical need to explain the fact of aesthetic repetition to a generation whose faith in originality was confronted by the (re)discovery of its very impossibility" (2007, par. 2). Randall views cultural recycling as a contemporary iteration of classical imitation, and she rightly identifies the literary turn toward recycling language through reappropriation as a response to changes in contemporary culture. Although Randall ultimately takes issue with the concept of cultural recycling, her realization that the popularity of recycling arises from contemporary culture's crisis of originality is not unlike Goldsmith's. He boldly proclaims that "living when technology is changing the rules of the game in every aspect of our lives, it's time to question and tear down such clichés [as creativity] and lay them out on the floor in front of us, then reconstruct these smoldering embers into something new, something contemporary, something—finally—relevant" (Goldsmith 2011, 9). Identifying twenty-first-century changes in how humans perceive the world, Goldsmith posits that artists must embrace the unoriginality embedded in that context and work to create or "reconstruct" something that is indeed "relevant" to the current social, historical, technological, and political moment.

## KENNETH GOLDSMITH'S (ECO)POETICS

Goldsmith puts his methodology of unoriginality into action in his own poetry. Beginning with a poetics of recording and copying, in *Fidget* (2000) he transcribes his own movements for a day; in *Soliloquy* (2001) the poet records all of the words he says or hears for a week; and *Day* (2003) is a copied volume of the *New York Times* into the form of a book. In all of these projects, the poet engages in an uncreative poetics, simply recording and copying without creating original text. However, his more recent books, ranging from the trilogy of *The Weather* (2005), *Traffic* (2007), and *Sports* (2008) to his most recent, *Seven American Deaths and Disasters*, engage even more radically in the process of appropriation central to new-century poetics by pulling texts in their entirety from original sources and placing them in the poetic context.

For Goldsmith, this poetics is a responsible and sustainable practice through which the poet can take words that are already in existence and give them new meaning. In "Being Boring," he explains the motivation behind his appropriation: "In 1969, the conceptual artist Douglas Huebler wrote, 'The world is full of objects, more or less interesting; I do not wish to add any more.' I've come to embrace Huebler's ideas, though it might be retooled as, 'The world is full of texts, more or less interesting; I do not wish to add any more'" (Goldsmith 2004, par. 3).

His intention not "to add any more" texts to the world but rather to recycle those that are already in existence is a fundamentally environmental impulse, yet the poet gets ecocritical attention only indirectly in terms of waste studies. Considering the overwhelming amount of language that confronts individuals on a daily basis in his waste studies approach to Goldsmith, Christopher Schmidt argues that "Goldsmith reminds us that few consumers read *every* word of the newspaper, even in its original format.... We skim, we skip, and read only the bits of interest, ignoring vast amounts of primary and secondary information (page numbers, story jumps, bylines) to avoid wasting time" (Schmidt 2014, 132). Approaching Goldsmith's poetics from the perspective of waste studies raises interesting questions about how appropriation functions and why it is useful. However, the poet is not read specifically for his attention to recycling or reworking to reveal new insights. Just as a recycling center turns plastic bottles into everything from reusable coffee cups to paint, buildings, car interiors, headphones, and even bridges, Goldsmith's poetics takes words that are largely ignored in their current form and makes them fresh, useful, and relevant to a new moment. This sentiment echoes Susan Signe Morrison's conception of waste.[4] She contends that "compost aesthetics reads poetry that acknowledges the poignancy of materiality" and "poetry, itself inherently metaphorical, functions as a kind of homeopathy or social cure for the alienation and disgust we all too often feel toward our own and others' bodily and material waste and decay" (Morrison 2015, 13). Put another way, employing cultural waste in poetry, as Goldsmith does, provides insight into cultural attitudes toward waste and perhaps acts to alter those perspectives by reappropriating and indeed reinjecting value into the detritus of human life. Similarly, in her chapter on Goldsmith, Perloff explores the poet's process of appropriation and observes that through its redeployment "a device obsolete in one period can be restaged and reframed at a different moment and in a different context and once again made 'perceptible'" (2010, 20). The process of recycling or appropriating material allows Goldsmith to give those texts that are seemingly obsolete and irrelevant to the contemporary reader new significance as it recontextualizes them for new challenges, problems, and concerns. In terms of unnatural ecopoetics, Goldsmith's methodology presents the promise of a fully self-conscious and self-reflexive textual space that enacts environmentality by emerging from the physical, cultural, and personal unfolding of particular experiences.

However, the significance of Goldsmith's appropriation poetics has undergone and continues to undergo debate among poets and literary critics. The poet has gained popularity in contemporary poetry circles, appearing in Perloff's recent book and releasing his own revolutionary critical text, *Uncreative Writing*. Much of the criticism on his work appears in a 2005 issue of the Canadian journal *Open Letter*, dedicated specifically to Goldsmith and conceptual poetics. In this issue, scholars and poets like Craig Dworkin, Christian Bök, Marjorie Perloff, Joshua Schuster, and Molly Schwartzburg write on Goldsmith's avant-garde poetics. In these articles, interpretations of Goldsmith's work vary dramatically. For instance, in "Encyclopedic Novelties: On Kenneth

Goldsmith's Tomes," Molly Schwartzburg argues that Goldsmith's books are as much about if not more about his own experience making them as they are about the moments they purport to represent (2005, 33). This critic identifies the poet's own composition process as the takeaway from his work. While others, like Christian Bök, view his work as a larger commentary on the present state of poetry. In "A Silly Key: Some Notes on *Soliloquy* by Kenneth Goldsmith," Bök posits that Goldsmith's employment of everyday speech comments on both past oversights and new directions for poetic discourse. He observes that "Goldsmith attacks the literary pretense of such common speech, demonstrating that lyric poets who purport to speak in the vernacular do not in fact do so because they do not, halfway through a thought, stutter words or corrupt ideas, neither repeating themselves nor redacting themselves" (2005, 63). In this statement, Bök implies that Goldsmith's poetry engages with the raw, unmediated, unpolished language of everyday speech, encapsulating the reality of that experience in the poem. Several years later, similar ideas are expressed in Schmidt's article on Goldsmith, which considers the connections between the poet's work and the increasingly popular waste studies movement by looking at two early books, *Fidget* and *Soliloquy*. He observes that Goldsmith engages in a "productive tension between efficiency and waste" in his writing (2008, 27). While the concept of waste has gained popularity since the publication of the *Open Letter* special issue, Schmidt's identification of wasted language in contemporary culture is remarkably similar to Bök's uncovering of the oversight of the ugly realities of everyday speech.

Since the publication of these articles, though, Goldsmith's work has shifted rather dramatically as he has turned toward transcription. Yet *Traffic* and *The Weather* continue to be the texts in Goldsmith's oeuvre that receive substantial critical attention. Marjorie Perloff writes of *The Weather* that it "is a work of radical defamiliarization. It forces the reader to think about the weather in entirely new ways" (Perloff 2005, 82). For Perloff, Goldsmith's poetics "exemplifies the powers of 'mere' transcription, mere copying, to produce new meanings" (2005, 77). Goldsmith is not simply being "uncreative" but, she argues, is forwarding new ideas through this experimental approach. Certainly, the poet's early books yield this insight about the power of transcription. Yet, *Seven American Deaths and Disasters*, a similar project of appropriation yet one rife with complications of cultural dialogue, multiple sources, and emotional investment, and arguably Goldsmith's most progressive book, has not drawn much critical attention. Transcribing radio and television reports of selected nationally significant deaths and disasters, Goldsmith creates a poetic expression of lived experiences by placing side by side the various cultural depictions that arose with the events themselves and emphasizing how the broadcasts influence conceptions of the events. In appropriated or found poems like Goldsmith's, language is extracted directly from cultural iterations of lived experience in media; unnatural ecopoetics reveals that the poet draws the material and nonmaterial elements from the broadcasts and foregrounds the many elements that shape experience—cultural, digital, natural, and political. As Goldsmith transcribes reports from particular experiences in the world, he expresses those cultural moments in text and reveals the complexity of lived moments. As the poet explains in his "Technical Notes," the transcriptions are sourced differently—some come from a single source and others are compilations of a variety of broadcasts (2013, 174–75). In pulling broadcasts into the textual space and sometimes splicing them together, Goldsmith recontextualizes those moments and redeploys them for a new purpose.

Still, what makes Goldsmith's book ecopoetic? Entirely uninterested in traditional representations of nature, *Seven American Deaths and Disasters* is an unlikely example for an ecopoetic reading and seemingly a less direct specimen than Goldsmith's other books—namely *The Weather*, which has clear environmental undertones in its consideration of how environmental elements are perceived, represented, and responded to in everyday life. Yet, *Seven American Deaths and Disasters* is not as far removed from new understandings of environment as might appear. The new materialist ideas and concepts of new spaces that are discussed in the introduction to this book have altered understandings of environment to include the types of spaces that make up Goldsmith's project. In a sense, Goldsmith's work embodies Henri Lefebvre's contention that "we are...confronted by an indefinite multitude of spaces, each one piled upon, or perhaps contained within, the next: geographical, economic, demographic, sociological, ecological, political, commercial, national, continental, global. Not to mention nature's (physical) space, the space of (energy) flows, and so on" (Lefebvre 1991, 8). In Goldsmith's book, these various spaces are thrust together within a textual space—one in which the environmentality of a lived moment is represented in text. Goldsmith's fusion of various spaces reveals how different kinds of spaces come together to compose an environmental experience.

In *Seven American Deaths and Disasters*, at least three levels of space exist: the physical space (the event itself) is fused and arguably shaped by the cultural space (the media's coverage amid everyday radio chatter), and those layers are further complicated by their reproduction in the textual space of Goldsmith's book, which acknowledges that all experiences are shaped by the cultural conversations that depict them and in turn foregrounds the cultural space through the book's found form.[5] It is in the fusion of these three spaces that Goldsmith's ecopoetics emerges. Depicting particular moments in time through their highly mediated representations in media and foregrounding the poet's intervention in reproducing such representations, Goldsmith's poetics reflects the event itself in a way that is conscious of the layers of perception and language that mediate poetry's reproduction of lived experience. Goldsmith's ecopoetics does not emerge from the depiction of natural or even physical environments but instead through the journalistic expression of a lived moment, which exists in our minds based on the *ways* we experienced it. Since most Americans were not physically present at the place and time of these seven monumental deaths and disasters, they understand, imagine, and process them through cultural sources of media along with their own physical and mental space and time. Thus, the lived experience is not only environmental or physical, but composed of a variety of spaces at once.

In this way, *Seven American Deaths and Disasters* engages to a radical degree with unnatural environments and lends itself to unnatural ecopoetics because of its interest in environmentality (and the many spaces that compose it) rather than mimesis. In the first chapter, on John F. Kennedy's death, the physical space of the event itself is deeply embedded within the cultural space of media. In one of the first appearances of the disaster in the text, the poem reads:

> May we suggest you stock up for the weekend with Texas brewed premium Hamm's beer at popular Texas prices. Refreshing as a glass of water, that's the taste, fresh taste of Hamm's.
>
> Hey, be sure that you stock up for this weekend with Texas-brewed premium Hamm's beer at popular Texas prices.
>
> And now we take you to KLIF Mobile Unit No. 4 in downtown Dallas.
>
> The latest information—and things are rather confused at this moment—shots definitely were fired at the presidential motorcade as it passed through downtown Dallas. All squads are converging code three in that area of Elm and Houston in downtown. There is a tentative description of the shooting suspect. A man, a white male believed to be approximately thirty years old, reportedly armed with a thirty caliber rifle. How many shots were fired, how many persons, if any, were struck and wounded, we do not know yet. Very closed-mouthed officials are

clamping down on the entire story. We'll bring you what details are available just as quickly as they come into our possession.

Sandra Dee has her troubles. Listen. A lot's been said about the wild teenage thing. But wait till you see the scrapes my dad Jimmy Stewart gets into. Yikes! (2013, 14–15)

Information on the event itself is revealed slowly throughout the chapter. Since the reports are recorded as information emerges on the events of the day, the broadcasters can only reveal "what details are available." Readers are thus granted access to the news as it unfolds rather than after the outcome has been learned and revealed to the public. What is perhaps most interesting about this passage, though, is the information that accompanies reports of the shooting. Aware of the possibility of tragedy, listeners await further details while listening to beer advertisements and film publicity. As the text moves from selling "Hamm's beer" to the news that "shots definitely were fired" and finally on to promoting Jimmy Stewart's latest film, it juxtaposes the various aspects of culture that contextualize and shape conceptions of physical reality.

Elsewhere in the book, Goldsmith discusses the material added to an original event or physical space, contemplating electronic data added to his e-mail of a nursery rhyme. He considers this added material "linguistic marks left by the network ecology" and argues in *Uncreative Writing* that "the new texts… [are] of equal importance to the nursery rhyme. Identifying the sources of those texts and noting their subsequent impact is part of the reading and writing experience" (2011, 31). Through what Goldsmith considers "network ecology," or a system of digital forces that interact and shape one another, content is changed as it is digitized. In essence, he claims that the processes through which the original is transported or expressed leaves "linguistic marks" that alter the original, but these additions are valuable contributions to the experience of the text. In the poem, there are arguably two layers of these marks: first, the advertisements, songs, commentary, and other information that is added to the reports of the physical event of JFK's death; second, the marks left by the transcription process as the poet selects and organizes the broadcast for the textual space. In essence, Goldsmith's conception of "network ecology" is similar to the tenets of unnatural ecopoetics, in that it recognizes or even foregrounds the changes to original material or experiences throughout the process of perception and reexpression.

The first of these "linguistic marks" alters conceptions of the event itself, as the added material frames JFK's death within the context of reality and fiction. The beer advertisement prompts individuals to "stock up for the weekend" on

Hamm's beer, as an escape from reality, and the broadcast proceeds through the shooting and immediately into publicity for Jimmy Stewart's film *Take Her, She's Mine* (1963). The reader is, then, faced with the fiction of momentary escape, confronted with the stark reality of the shooting, and immediately thrust back into the fiction of a film. This material contextualizes the event, ultimately altering perceptions of the shooting. The second of these "linguistic marks" appears formally in the poet's transcription. The harsh juxtapositions of reality and fiction are not marked by formal, textual, or stylistic shifts. All the sections appear identical, with no distinguishing between the real and the imagined. The lack of distinguishing marks emphasizes the book's textual nature and even positions it as a metatextual work, which, as Michael Kaufmann puts it in *Textual Bodies: Modernism, Postmodernism, and Print*, "break[s] up the print rectangle of the page and make[s] the physical form of the book 'visible' to expose print conventions and the effect of print on language" (1994, 14). Goldsmith's book is metatextual both for its foregrounding of the marks left by the transcription, through the poet's choices to begin and end in particular places in the original broadcast, and the marks left by the broadcast on conceptions of the event itself. The two types of "linguistic marks" evident in the book, then, reveal the ways in which cultural and physical space are deeply intertwined and simultaneously foreground the textual space through which those connections are exposed. Reading *Seven American Deaths and Disasters* through the lens of unnatural ecopoetics reveals how the hyper-inauthenticity of the textual space highlights the cultural, historical, and personal factors that shape experience.

Goldsmith's deployment of language and form are similarly central to his ecopoetics. Transcribing text directly rather than creating new commentary on the events works alongside developments in contemporary consciousness and foregrounds the limitations of the poem's form. By moving a real-world event into the poem via the cultural dialogue that it generated, the poem highlights the language and form of the event's release to the public and thus foregrounds its textuality. The act of moving the broadcast to the page raises the reader's awareness of the words as text with agential power. The words are not simply reporting information, but are shaping the way the reader perceives and understands the physical event. In this sense, Goldsmith's reappropriation and recontextualization of the broadcasts raises the reader's awareness of their cultural impact. Vanessa Place and Robert Fitterman observe that "conceptual writing mediates between the written object (which may or may not be a text) and the meaning of the object by framing the writing as a figural object to be narrated.... In this way, conceptual writing creates an object that creates

its own disobjectification" (2009, 15–16). For this discussion, Place and Fitterman's point implies that the book takes the broadcast and wrings out the meaning of it through "disobjectification" or denaturalization. Moving the broadcast
from its original moment to the page demands close examination of the words
as words and ultimately reveals the multiple ways that words function.

The ways in which the poet facilitates these engagements with space are
masked behind the book's concept of "uncreative writing." While it may seem
impossible for the poet to express his own purpose through the seemingly
unoriginal act of transcription, the book actually includes a number of telling creative moments in which Goldsmith's ecopoetic purpose peeks through.
In *Uncreative Writing*, he claims that "the suppression of self-expression is
impossible. Even when we do something as seemingly 'uncreative' as retyping a few pages, we express ourselves in a variety of ways. The act of choosing
and reframing tells us as much about ourselves as our story about our mother's
cancer operation" (2011, 9). Even in transcription, the poet expresses himself
and forwards a particular message. In *Seven American Deaths and Disasters*,
this self-expression appears at the edges in the poet's choice of events, careful
decisions of where to begin and end each section, and in simple choices like
where to insert paragraph breaks. By closely analyzing these elements of the
book, we can begin to interpret not only the messages of the broadcasts, but
even more importantly, Goldsmith's experiences. Through the poet's expression of the various elements that compose his real-world experience and his
exposure of the edges or constructedness of the text, he reveals that the book
does not represent cultural moments or particular environments in isolation;
Goldsmith's unnatural ecopoetics enacts a self-conscious deployment of environmentality through which subjective experiences—physical, cultural, and
personal—are granted significance. Unnatural ecopoetics reveals that Goldsmith's book is not simply an uncreative or unoriginal rendering of events, but
an acknowledgment of how the poet's (and even reader's) experiences contribute to environmentality at least as much as the physical event or environment
being expressed.

The poet's subjectivity may initially seem difficult to identify in *Seven
American Deaths and Disasters* because of the work's found form. Yet, the
poet's self-expression is apparent in the book through his choice of events.
The chapters cover John F. Kennedy, Robert F. Kennedy, John Lennon, the
space shuttle *Challenger*, Columbine High School, the World Trade Center, and
Michael Jackson. The choice to include Michael Jackson but not Martin Luther
King Jr. seems particularly unusual, but Goldsmith explains in his afterword
that he chose events "based on the fact that they were unraveling in real time,

thus highlighting the broadcasters' uncertainty as to what they were actually describing" (2013, 174). The prioritizing of the "broadcasters' uncertainty" over the social, cultural, and historical significance of the events themselves suggests that the poet's purpose is not simply to present important moments from recent history for the reader's nostalgic remembrance but rather to encourage critical examination of the ways in which events are shaped by their telling. The ways that the physical events in the broadcasts are altered by the broadcasts that depict them will be discussed in detail in the coming pages, but it is important to first consider what the poet's prioritizing of uncertainty over significance implies. The uncertainty with which the news is broadcast appears to be tied to the poet's decisions over where to begin and end each section. What is arguably the least "certain" broadcast in the book, the John F. Kennedy section, begins with a loaded and entirely uncontextualized line: "See The Wheeler Dealers" (2013, 9). After moving past this unusual opening to the book, the reader discovers that *The Wheeler Dealers* is a film. Goldsmith's decision to begin the book with an advertisement for a film initially seems innocuous but actually reveals an important message that runs throughout much of the text. Foregrounding the presence of advertisements at the beginning of the book emphasizes the ways in which cultural elements shape physical spaces. The poet's unnatural ecopoetics in this section, then, is evident in his framing of the physical event (the assassination) with the cultural elements of the advertisement and the broadcast itself because it demonstrates that the physical events of the disasters are dramatically altered by being embedded within advertisements. Through this lens, readers become hyperaware of the constructedness of the telling, which does not diminish the effectiveness of Goldsmith's rendering of Kennedy's death; rather, it arguably makes it more real to the average reader by prompting him to consider and acknowledge his distance from the physical event itself and the artificiality inherent in his understanding of it.

The poet's decisions about which broadcasts to transcribe are similarly expository of his self-expression. In the John Lennon section of the book, the text is radically foregrounded when Goldsmith transcribes "a cassette tape of a radio scan someone made by flipping through the radio dial on the evening of December 8, 1980," which is followed by "a variety of airchecks" (2013, 175). Unlike in the section on John F. Kennedy, the coverage of John Lennon is further complicated by the fusion of a variety of sources, each entirely uncontextualized:

> An unspeakable tragedy confirmed to us by ABC News in New York City. John Lennon, outside of his apartment building on the West Side

of New York City, the most famous perhaps of all the Beatles, shot twice
in the back, rushed to Roosevelt Hospital, dead on arrival. Hard to go
back to the game after that newsflash. Frank Gifford?
　　Indeed it is.
　　...for scenes on December tenth, 1938, the first scenes from the
film Gone With the Wind. The burning of Atlanta sequence lights the
sky for miles...
　　We interrupt this program to bring you a special bulletin from
NBC News. Former Beatle John Lennon is dead. Lennon died in a hospital shortly after being shot outside his New York apartment tonight.
(2013, 73)

In jumping from one station to the next, this transcription emphasizes the multiple channels through which language finds the listener and shapes his or her
conceptions of the world. Each station provides a different language that influences how one understands the event, and the listener's conception of it is further complicated by the unrelated cultural data that accompanies the reports
("scenes from the film Gone With the Wind" and "the game"). In this sense, the
reports of Lennon's death are accompanied by "linguistic marks" or additional
data that influence the listener. The book, though, takes this a step further by
placing the confused and jumbled reports in a sequence on the page in which
stations are not distinguished from one another and reports on the death are
seamlessly attached to reports on football and film.
　　By pulling the radio broadcasts to the page, Goldsmith highlights the limitations of words. The words do not simply serve as portals for information but
are themselves significant in shaping the moment. As Perloff writes, "this is a
poetry that conceives of the poem as meaning-making machine and takes its
motive from what Adorno termed *resistance*: the resistance of the individual
poem to the larger cultural field of capitalist commodification where language
has become merely instrumental" (2010, 9). Goldsmith's poems are "meaning-
making machine[s]" precisely because he removes the language from its original context and use, making it not "merely instrumental" but formative. In
the language presented in the book a textual space is formed; this is a place
in which a variety of spaces converge to produce a complex environment. By
creating a textual space where language is emphasized as language and not
a pseudo-authentic expression of an original moment or object, Goldsmith
demonstrates the permanently mediated effects of language, effects that are
further emphasized throughout the book by its constant intermingling of real
and imagined or physical and cultural moments.

An unnatural ecopoetic reading of the book makes evident the poet's push to acknowledge the hyper-inauthenticity of the tellings, which grows from the subjectivity of experience, the authorial incursions in the text, and the cultural influence on each section, and demonstrates the value that comes with the text's infusion of multiple spaces. Through the lens of unnatural ecopoetics, it is clear that for Goldsmith, the interplay of various spaces on the page make tangible experiences, moments, or even events by recognizing the many elements that constitute environmentality. He writes: "By taking our city's physical geography and overlaying it with *psychogeography*—a technique of mapping the psychic and emotional flows of a city instead of its rational street grids—we become more sensitive to our surroundings" (2011, 37; emphasis in original). The same concept can be applied to *Seven American Deaths and Disasters* by thinking about the physical space as inclusive of the events in the book. Those physical spaces are overlaid with the "psychic and emotional" spaces that accompany them. By fusing those spaces in the text, the ways in which they overlap become particularly apparent to the reader, ultimately foregrounding the complex and multifaceted environments that compose experience. The ways in which various spaces overlap and influence one another is particularly apparent in the section on the World Trade Center, which begins:

> This just in. You are looking at obviously a very disturbing live shot there. That is the World Trade Center, and we have unconfirmed reports this morning that a plane has crashed into one of the towers of the World Trade Center.
>
> We are right now just beginning to work on this story, obviously calling our sources and trying to figure out exactly what happened. But clearly, something relatively devastating happening this morning here on the south end of the island of Manhattan.
>
> This is, once again, a picture of one of the towers of the World Trade Center.
>
> And as we can see in these pictures, obviously something devastating that has happened. And again, there are unconfirmed reports that a plane has crashed into one of the towers there. We are efforting more information in the subject as it becomes available to you. (2013, 127)

The World Trade Center disaster leads the book into recent history, to a moment that most living Americans recall with great sadness. Yet, it is an event that the American people learned of primarily through radio and television reports rather than through personal experience. The disconnection between the physical event and the culturally constructed mental and emotional space in which the majority of people experienced it makes this disaster particularly illustrative of the power that appropriation holds. The poet highlights the disconnection between the event itself and the broadcasts of it when he explains in his afterword that as he watched as the towers of the World Trade Center crumbled, he listened to "an AM radio station that was narrating the very events [he] was witnessing. There was a strange disconnect—a feeling of simulacra and spectacle—as if this show had been planned and presented the way that, say, reality television had recently begun to permeate our lives" (2013, 171). The disconnection that the poet identifies between the reality of the moment and the telling of it on the radio is precisely what is expressed through the textual space of the poem. In other words, the unnatural ecopoetics of the book lies in its insistence that readers remain cognizant of the inherent artificiality of language and the unavoidable gap between a text and physical reality. As Goldsmith draws the broadcast of this epic disaster into the textual space, the reader becomes aware of his or her distance from the physical event itself and is reminded of the methods by which he or she formulated mental and emotional constructions of it.

Goldsmith exaggerates the distance from which most Americans experienced the World Trade Center disaster by emphasizing the uncertainty in the reports that irreversibly shaped cultural consciousness of the event. The section begins with the report's tentative and immediate nature ("This just in"), immediately informing the reader of the report's ambiguous character and limited information. The broadcaster begins, though, not by explaining that the information comes from "unconfirmed reports" but instead by referring to the "disturbing" nature of an image or "shot." When the report is pulled into the textual space, it is clear that by beginning with the commentary on the "disturbing" event even before informing the listener of its tentative nature, listeners are immediately inscribed with the event's horror. Of course, the event itself is disturbing and horrific, but Goldsmith's appropriation of the text and his decision to begin the section in this way foregrounds the language through which the nation's experience of this event was formulated.

Not present to witness the event for themselves, the listeners had their conceptions of it irreversibly shaped by the broadcast. In large part, this is the product of the broadcaster's uncertainty. As he attempts to comment only on what he sees, he restates the obvious nature of the images ("obviously a very disturbing live shot," "clearly, something relatively devastating happening," and "obviously something devastating"). Decontextualized from the fear and devastation of the event itself through its placement in the textual space, the broadcaster's tone of fear and uncertainty are central to national sentiments surrounding the tragedy. Newspaper headlines from September 12, 2001, express similar feelings of "devastation" and "terror" as well as "terrifying" feelings and thoughts of the act's "unthinkable" nature.[6] Although these headlines were printed after much more information was released, and certainly do not definitively show that this single broadcast shaped perceptions of the tragedy, they do reveal that the uncertainty, fear, and disbelief expressed by the broadcaster in Goldsmith's transcription was present in national sentiments about the disaster. When viewed in the poetic context, Goldsmith's book reveals how the words that publicized the World Trade Center disaster shaped conceptions, responses, and emotional investment in the event itself. In other words, the discourse in which the event was narrated not only told the story but shaped it.

Twelve years after the tragedy, the poet's appropriation of this broadcast into the textual space distances the reader from the physical experience of the event in order to encourage critical thinking about how cultural, mental, and historical spaces influence overall conceptions of 9/11. It is the fusion of these various elements both on the part of the broadcaster and the individual listeners that constructs the tragedy. While the physical space is devastating in itself, only when the physical space intersects with a variety of other elements does the physical gain significance. In the same section of his book, Goldsmith reiterates the power that the cultural space wields over conceptions of the event when the report suddenly cuts to traffic:

> We thank you very much for your insight. Why don't we take a quick look at traffic. Debbie, I'm sure traffic has got to be a mess. Debbie, are you there?
> Yes I am. Um, traffic is a nightmare. All the bridges and tunnels getting into the city are being shut down right now. Lincoln, Holland, George. Shut. Forget about it. Turn around. Go back home. Fifty-ninth Street Bridge. Closed. Brooklyn Bridge, Williamsburg, Brooklyn Battery Tunnel, again the Manhattan Bridge, uh, everything being closed heading into the city. And of course you want to avoid the area of the Twin Towers right now. You have tons of emergency vehicles there. And also all the area airports are closed, uh, Newark, Kennedy, LaGuardia, all the major airports are shut down. So again, avoid this area of the city. It is a nightmare. (2013, 136)

The unexpected shift to traffic here is reminiscent of Goldsmith's earlier book, *Traffic*, in which the transcription of traffic broadcasts reveals the extent to which traffic dictates the patterns of everyday life in the city. In his earlier book, the poet implies that transportation has consumed contemporary existence to the point that everything else is dictated by the traffic. The broadcaster's turn to regularly scheduled segments during the coverage of 9/11 reveals the ways in which cultural elements are privileged or at least considered equal to material reality in contemporary society. Used to a particular schedule for the show, even when faced with an unprecedented disaster, the broadcaster engages in the mundane cultural dialogue of traffic and in the following paragraph an oddly ineffective warning to his television audience about television broadcast unavailability (2013, 136). The broadcaster's impulse to report news even when it is irrelevant to the situation or the audience demonstrates the power of cultural space even in the midst of a pressing event in one's physical surroundings.

The sudden turn to traffic in the midst of the Twin Towers tragedy is unexpected and seemingly out of place and includes unusual if largely irrelevant and unnecessary details on the traffic problems across the city. Debbie's use of the word "nightmare" twice throughout the segment not in reference to the Twin Towers disaster but to traffic reveals a particular insensitivity to or perhaps disengagement from the tragedy at hand. By calling the traffic, a comparatively insignificant detail of the day, a "nightmare" in the circumstances of the real-life "nightmare" of the attack, Debbie reveals the equal importance of cultural space and physical space in today's society. Although the physical disaster of the Twin Towers is a pressing concern, the broadcaster's depiction of the cultural—the city's traffic flow—as nightmarish reveals that regardless of the outcome, the two are equally important. The physical does not take precedence over the cultural space; rather, both exist simultaneously in the broadcast.

Similarly, her needless reporting of seemingly obvious information like the closure of bridges, tunnels, and airports is exacerbated by the unnecessary detail of listing which venues are closed ("All of the bridges and tunnels getting into the city are being shut down right now. Lincoln, Holland, George. Shut. Forget about it"). After indicating that "all of the bridges and tunnels" are closed, Debbie continues to list specific closures and then wittily tells listeners to "forget about it" and "turn around." She similarly warns listeners to "avoid the area of the Twin Towers" and explains that "all the area airports are closed," but then proceeds to list them by name ("Newark, Kennedy, LaGuardia, all the major airports are shut down"). Providing repetitive and unnecessary details, the broadcaster discloses the sense of confusion plaguing the nation but simultaneously demonstrates the instinctual turn in contemporary society toward prescribed cultural frames. In his review of Goldsmith's book, Dwight Garner of the *New York Times* writes, "His book is about the sounds our culture makes when the reassuring smooth jazz of much of our broadcast media breaks down, when disc jockeys and news anchors are forced to find words for events that are nearly impossible to describe. This book is about language under duress" (2013, par. 7). By framing the disaster through the traffic problems plaguing the city and providing the inconsequential details of those problems, the horror of the day is made more ordinary, more acceptable, and more easily processed. If the broadcasters report closures, traffic, and outages as they do daily, the attack is perhaps less real and less frightening. The unnatural ecopoetics of the scene lies in its insistence on the mundane and emphasis on the uncertainty, fear, and confusion in the cultural depiction of real-world events. By highlighting the subjectivity in the cultural narrative, the poem exposes that language has the ability to shape real-world events in the minds of listeners and thus maintains a textual space all its own.

In the book, the newscasters' avoidance of the real physical event, which is facilitated by the traffic report, is challenged a few paragraphs later when the trivial is juxtaposed with the serious. The transcription of the broadcast cuts from traffic reports to television signals and finally to people jumping from the building. In these shifts, Goldsmith's poem shows the unreality of the television report, and the superficiality of its segments confronts reality as real people in the building jump to their deaths. As the broadcaster shows images of the World Trade Center, he comments:

> It is a terrible scene. People are just walking down the street with their hands covering their mouth in disbelief. They can't believe it. And then you hear the sirens and people screaming as they look up at the building and see people trying to get out and some people jumping. Now, the EMS is here, fire personnel, police, everyone's here trying to keep calm and get everyone away from the building and keep it safe. Let's listen.
> …but, um, I did see someone jump. I did. And I talked to someone and in her own voice you could hear it and she just lost it…
> …they…they're throwing themselves off the building. Oh my God.
> (2013, 136–37)

The broadcaster begins by remarking on the scene with relative objectivity and composure. He narrates the terror of the image and explains that "some people [are] jumping." However, the broadcast then begins to listen to an unspecified source who reignites the true horror of the scene when he or she hesitates to explain that the people in the building "they…they're throwing themselves off the building." Although the poet does not clarify whether the source has changed in this segment, it is clear that the poem has jumped from the television broadcaster to someone more deeply enmeshed in the scene— perhaps a firefighter or policeman. By juxtaposing the tone of the broadcaster who represents the cultural dialogue that illustrates, explains, and informs the public of the disaster with the commentary of an individual enmeshed in the physical event itself, Goldsmith highlights the ways in which depictions of events and experiences of physical events are often extremely different. What is perhaps most interesting about this, though, is that the broadcaster, the disconnected voice in the above passages, is the voice that the majority of the nation relies on for information; national opinions and conceptions of the World Trade Center disaster are formulated through his highly mediated and arguably skewed telling of it. This cultural space of the media shapes public conceptions of the physical events of the disaster. In highlighting the influence of culture and personal experience, Goldsmith employs an unnatural ecopoetics that insists on the hyper-inauthenticity of the text in order to expose the constant influence of personal and cultural elements on environmental experience.

## CONCLUSION

By drawing media broadcasts into the textual space, *Seven American Deaths and Disasters* allows readers to look into the various elements that compose environmentality. The textual space foregrounds the presence of multiple spaces by placing a cultural document of familiar national disasters on a page, which demands close reading, critical analysis, deep consideration, and theorization. Once the broadcasts become poems, they are viewed in a different light from their original format. The reader of the poem is looking for irregularities, problems, contradictions, and connections that the radio listener in the moment does not recognize. As Harold Bloom writes, "Language, to a considerable extent, is concealed figuration: ironies and synecdoches, metonymies and metaphors that we recognize only when our awareness increases. Real poetry is aware of and exploits these ruined tropes" (Bloom 2004, 5). While Bloom might not recognize Goldsmith's work as "real poetry," *Seven American Deaths and Disasters* engages in the "concealed figuration" that he identifies by ironically appropriating a highly mediated cultural document to illustrate the variety of spaces that influence the ways individuals experience particular moments or events. Reading Goldsmith's book in this way is to see that there is no national experience of the disasters included in the book, only individual ones. The experience is subjective, shaped by a variety of factors including the mental space, memories, emotional investment, location, distractions, and the cultural dialogue through which the individual learns of the event. The lens of unnatural ecopoetics reveals that Goldsmith's book foregrounds textual space through its conceptual form and within that space, exposing the intertwining of material and nonmaterial elements of human experience and the agential power that they hold over conceptions of reality.

Goldsmith's extraction of broadcasts from a variety of disasters into the textual space foregrounds the diverse ways in which individuals encounter those events. The book makes it clear that the cultural space is irreversibly tied to how individuals experience the physical space and that the two are always intertwined. Goldsmith, who is both an author and a teacher, often reflects in his book *Uncreative Writing* on interactions with his students. The poet acknowledges the subjectivity of experience when he comments, "the suppression of self-expression is impossible. Even when we do something as seemingly 'uncreative' as retyping a few pages, we express ourselves in a variety of ways," which leads his students to believe that the "uncreative" tasks assigned by the poet led to the most creative work they have ever produced (Goldsmith 2011, 9). His explanation of the diverse ways in which his students complete a seemingly uncreative project reveals the power in Goldsmith's poetics and the underlying sentiment of *Seven American Deaths and Disasters*. An unnatural ecopoetic approach to Goldsmith's book shows that individual experiences of particular moments are entirely subjective, always mediated by elements that are unique to each place, time, and person. Any attempt to express a real experience must account for this subjectivity and embrace the uncertainty inherent in any perception. An individual is bound to impose new information, select and exclude data, and imbue any encounter with his or her ideologies, experiences, memories, and agendas.

It is Goldsmith's recognition of both the material and nonmaterial elements of real-world experience and his willingness to foreground those elements in his poetry that makes his work an ideal text for unnatural ecopoetic critique. Unlike earlier conceptions of ecopoetics, unnatural ecopoetics specifically engages poetics like Goldsmith's, which foregrounds the complex interrelation of material and nonmaterial aspects of experience. Some critics may argue that *Seven American Deaths and Disasters* is not an ecopoem and should not be considered for ecopoetic critique because of its lack of attention to the natural world. Indeed, Goldsmith's work is uninterested in the natural environment, but like the poetics of Lyn Hejinian, his is invested in an examination of perception, investigating the ways in which individuals experience the world around them. Goldsmith does not consider how a physical space is represented in text but rather examines the multiple spaces that compose a lived moment. That experience is not made up of only one type of perception but rather is influenced and shaped by personal elements of memory, mood, and individual investment as well as larger social factors such as cultural dialogue, history, politics, and physical space. Even within larger social events, each individual will recognize, prioritize, ignore, leave out, or emphasize particular facets of an encounter.

While ecopoetic theory does not often recognize the ways nonphysical spaces are manifested in poetry, reading Goldsmith's book through this lens demonstrates how ecopoetics can uncover new spaces and environments. In this way, ecopoetic critique is useful beyond blatantly green or even overtly environmental texts and becomes useful in considering space on a broad level. As Edward W. Soja writes, scholars must move away from the traditional duality of physical and imagined space for the realization that "*everything* comes together in Thirdspace: subjectivity and objectivity, the abstract and the concrete, the real and the imagined, the knowable and the unimaginable, the repetitive and the differential, structure and agency, mind and body, consciousness and the unconscious, the disciplined and the transdisciplinary, everyday life and unending history" (Soja 1996, 56–57; emphasis in original). This new open space allows ideas of environment to more readily engage with contemporary life. Space is not only the physical environment around us or the imagined place of the mind but a fusion of countless elements in between. For ecopoetics, this shift demonstrates that even in the least eco-oriented poetry, spaces are at the fore, interrelating in complex and surprising ways. It is in these unlikely spaces that ecopoetic theory can begin to expand beyond conceptions of environments as purely physical and begin to embrace their metaphysical elements with equal enthusiasm and importance. The shift toward these new spaces does not discount the real-world action demanded in much ecopoetic theory, but instead allows the field to embrace new types of activisms that are transnational, culturally diverse, and inclusive of a wide array of American poetry.

### NOTES

1. For a more detailed discussion of the history of appropriation in poetry, see Perloff's *Unoriginal Genius: Poetry by Other Means in the New Century*. In the book's introduction, she nicely relates contemporary appropriation poetry back to modernist traditions.

2. Although Kosuth's book was published in 2000, he began writing it in 1966. As Dworkin and Goldsmith point out in *Against Expression: An Anthology of Conceptual Writing*, "Kosuth directly applied precepts common during the 1960s heyday of conceptual art to writing, thus setting a precedent for conceptual writing strategies" (2011, 331).

3. The critique of culture is apparent in some works of appropriation, especially in the art world. Artists like Duchamp and Warhol certainly aim to critique the culture industry from which they emerge, but many appropriation poets, such as Goldsmith, Howe, and others, use appropriation to foreground the boundaries, complexities, and multiplicities of language.

4. Morrison explores this topic in her article "Waste Aesthetics: Form as Restitution," and then expands on her earlier ideas in her 2015 book, *The Literature of Waste: Material Ecopoetics and Ethical Matter.*

5. I would argue, however, that there are many more levels of space at work in the book. Other spaces that shape how humans conceive and understand events, like the historical space and perhaps subjective mental space, could also be considered.

6. "Devastation" comes from the *Baltimore Sun*. "Terrifying" was the headline in the *Oakland Tribune*. "Terror" appeared in the headlines of a variety of newspapers, including the *Arizona Republic*, the *Advocate*, and the *Seattle Times*. "Unthinkable" appeared as the headline in the *Salt Lake City Tribune*.

# The Future of Ecopoetics in New Poetries and New Spaces

I BEGAN WORKING on ecopoetics while living in Long Beach, California, a city engulfed by the highly urban space of Los Angeles. Ecopoetic theory, in the early 2000s, accounted for poetry that engages with nature, even urban nature, but the majority of my environment was unnatural, and ecopoetics had no way of dealing specifically with the built aspects of the city. While ecopoetics raised interesting questions about how environments make their way into poetry, it did not fully account for much of the poetry of the twentieth and twenty-first centuries, much of which lacks traditional nature and arises from entirely urban spaces, and all of which is deeply embedded within physical, textual, and personal space. Given this, it might seem easier to simply toss the term "ecopoetics" aside and conjure up something new that better accounts for a broader swath of contemporary poetry and other modes of experimental and lyrical language. But to do so would ignore the sense of environmental significance and formal engagement with space that ecopoetics has contributed to literary studies. The term "ecopoetics" is certainly evolving but should not be discounted because of its root, "eco." The concept of "eco" is itself changing, as we come to recognize the permeability of its borders—"ecological" does not simply point to trees, weeds, or beaches but extends into the recesses of the human body and the nuances of experiences in the material world. Instead of bolstering the dichotomy between "human" and "nature," what I'm calling "unnatural ecopoetics" recognizes movements in poetry and other forms of language to overcome this supposed gap through the textual space. Unnatural ecopoetics allows for the recognition of naturalcultural elements in a wide array of contemporary poetry, much of which has long been excluded from the realm of ecocriticism and had its environmentality marginalized or entirely ignored in poetry studies. An unnatural ecopoetics breaks away from the assumed parallel between "eco" and "natural" and moves toward naturalcultural conceptualizations of environment. The term uncovers how texts use self-reflexive language and formal experimentation to create a textual space where material and nonmaterial elements of environmentality are uncovered.

The shift to unnatural ecopoetics follows the trajectory of ecocritical theory, which has increasingly broadened its applications beyond texts with overtly natural content and challenged the constrictions within the idea of "nature." In its movement away from traditional conceptions of nature, my term "unnatural ecopoetics" responds to Timothy Morton's contention that "ecocriticism is too enmeshed in the ideology that churns out stereotypical ideas of nature to be of any use" (2007, 13). Morton's proclamation challenges ecocritics to address the problematic undertones of the word "nature," which he identifies as stereotyped because it is conceptualized as something that is other and "over there" rather than something that is ever-present in experience. At least in critical theory, the term "nature," although purporting to represent the physical world beyond language and ideology, is always wrapped up in the ideologies of the writer. When the word "nature" is deployed, the reader is exposed only to an artificial other and never looks at his or her own physical reality. At issue here are the environmental responsibilities that are overlooked when nature is viewed as something "over there" and when one fails to recognize that it is, in fact, all around. For ecocritics, this problem has arisen throughout subfields of material ecocriticism and environmental justice ecocriticism, through which scholars consider how striving for stereotypical ideas of "nature" has caused important real-world problems to be forgotten. As a result, these issues are regularly left out of "nature," making the term itself skewed by the ideology behind it. For Morton, the term "nature" prevents a meaningful relationship between human individuals and the physical world: "nature keeps giving writers the slip. And in all its confusing, ideological intensity, nature ironically impedes a proper relationship with the earth and its lifeforms, which would, of course, include ethics and science" (2007, 2). In pointing out that the term "nature" is impeding ethical and scientific relationships with the earth, Morton gestures toward the environmental concerns that lie beneath the surface of what is thought of as "nature" and touches on concerns within environmental justice movements for built spaces and the people within them. When writers allow the term "nature" to impede expressions of the naturalcultural reality of contemporary experiences, the word ceases to represent as intended and instead evokes a set of ideologically, historically, and even politically charged sentiments.

In the past decade, ecocritics have broadened their field by considering new genres and new types of environments, including urban environments. But even today there is, as evidenced by Morton's project, a great deal of concern over the distance between ideas of nature, often represented as disconnected from the urban experience familiar to much of the world's population, and reality. In her 2012 *PMLA* article on sustainability, "Beyond Imagining, Imagining Beyond," Lynn Keller contemplates how traditional conceptions of nature relate to the practical realities of contemporary life. She writes that "nature writing as it has developed from traditions of the pastoral contributes valuably to readers' appreciation of the given world…[yet] received ideas of nature codified in such writing tend, as many have noted, to position nature as something apart from the human, making it difficult to conceptualize ways for large populations to live appropriately in and with nature" (2012, 581). In other words, by placing value only on traditional concepts of nature, one ignores those places, and the people who live in them, where nature is tied up in human constructions rather than apart from them. Traditional writing about nature presents a similar risk; rather than demonstrating how individuals can connect to and appreciate their world, writing about "nature" demonstrates how distanced most individuals are from that natural world that is viewed as "over there," outside the boundaries of the city. By moving away from stereotyped "nature," as Morton suggests, ecocriticism can overcome ideologies that value one kind of space over another, a distinction that often results in environmental injustice because neighborhoods that are typically composed of poor racial minorities, when judged by the standard of "nature" as pastoral, wild, pure, and thus valuable, are viewed as less aesthetically pleasing, less valuable, and less in need of preservation or protection. Such sentiments are reiterated in the material turn in literary criticism and specifically in ecocriticism. As a result of critics such as Jane Bennett calling for increased attention to the power of things beyond the human realm, ecocriticism continues to broaden its reach to new literary landscapes. Propelling conventional ecopoetics toward unnatural ecopoetics contributes to this ongoing movement in ecocriticism by compelling critics to think through nature to more inclusive naturalcultural conceptions of environmentality.

The push toward environmentality responds to current trends in ecocritical scholarship. As ecocriticism embarks on its fourth wave, renewed interest in things troubles the boundaries between natural and unnatural or material and nonmaterial. Serenella Iovino and Serpil Oppermann present the concept of "material ecocriticism, [which] is the study of the way material forms— bodies, things, elements, toxic substances, chemicals, organic and inorganic manner, landscapes, and biological entities—intra-act with each other and with the human dimension, producing configurations of meanings and discourses that we can interpret as stories" (2014, 7). Pointing ecocritical theory toward acknowledging nonhuman agency and the importance of all forms of matter, material ecocriticism demands that critical perspectives account for the various elements in the universe that are always intra-acting and shaping one another. In doing so, material ecocriticism propels theory toward the sentiments of unnatural ecopoetics, which provides a critical lens that considers how those various elements are acknowledged and expressed textually. Coupled with the work of scholars like Scott Knickerbocker, Jonathan Skinner, and Brenda Iijima, who broaden the boundaries of ecopoetics, the concept of material eco-criticism represents an important bridge between ecocritical poetry studies and the changing view of what "nature" is and where its boundaries lie in con-temporary literary criticism. Unnatural ecopoetics builds on previous work in material ecocriticism and ecopoetics, bringing the two fields together by acknowledging naturecultures in unlikely spaces and broadening the reach of both fields into texts that are distinctly concerned with unnatural settings and cultural elements.

### THE FUTURE OF ECOPOETICS

Until now, ecopoetics has struggled to move beyond the search for remnants of nature in a poem. In doing so, it ignores the majority of environmental inter-actions, which are not distinctly natural. What makes ecopoetics so rigidly confined to traditional conceptions of nature even when ecocriticism has so clearly moved beyond such limitations? I present this question without a clear answer, but this book is my case for why and how ecopoetics can break through its prior usages and open up exciting new paths for ecocritical poetry studies. By removing the oft-assigned equivalency between ecological and natural and instead recognizing the environmentality of various kinds of spaces, even un-natural ones, we can look to new applications of ecopoetic theory in unlikely spaces. Unnatural ecopoetics illuminates how poems create a foregrounded textual space, using formal experimentation and self-reflexive language, where naturalcultural elements of environmental experiences are exposed and made active.

It is my hope that this book will inspire scholars to explore the possibilities of unnatural ecopoetics in bridging the gap that has long existed between eco-criticism and poetry studies. As I seek to demonstrate, while all poetry might be considered for its ecopoetic undertones, contemporary poetry is particu-larly suitable for such explorations in light of current ecocritical trends since these poets constantly challenge assumptions about what constitutes poetry and the limitations of space. Radical poets and artists like Robert Grenier, Christian Bök, and Patrick Haemmerlein play with medium and language to create works that straddle the boundaries between poetry, art, environment, and even biology, while writers like Vanessa Place present textual environments constructed on the boundary of poetry and prose and inundated with the influence of space.[1] These texts, although not all poetry and, for many readers, contestable examples of ecopoetry, are fundamentally interested in how form and language work together to express the naturalcultural elements of environmentality within the textual space. As unnatural ecopoetics continues to develop, it will provide a critical lens through which literary scholars can consider how environment, text, and personal experience fuse in art as they do in real-world experiences. The future of ecopoetics, in fact, demands looking beyond traditional iterations of environments and recognizing the environmentality of naturalcultural fusions, even when those fusions are subtly expressed.

Bök, for instance, who is perhaps best known for his exploration of "living poetry" through the injection of text into a sequence of DNA in the Xenotext Experiment, presents a poetics uniquely intertwined with the physical world through his union of poetry and science. Making biology a site for poetics, Bök's work presents new challenges for poetry studies and ecopoetics alike. His premise, though, is entirely environmental, as the experiment itself hinges on the possibility of "extend[ing] poetry itself beyond the formal limits of the book" and into the world beyond the page (Bök 2008, 230). Approaching his experiment through the lens of unnatural ecopoetics allows readers to acknowledge the environmentality of the text regardless of its medium. While the poet reaches beyond the traditional realms of text and nature, his poem is arguably as natural as poetry can ever be since "when translated into a gene and then integrated into the cell, the text nevertheless gets 'expressed' by the organism, which, in response to this grafted, genetic sequence, begins to manufacture a viable, benign protein—a protein that, according to the original, chemical alphabet, is itself another text" (2008, 229). The organism produces a text, a poetic space within a living creature. The poet's experiment uses textual play and formal experimentation to literally reveal naturalcultural fusions within the textual space—in this case, the organism expresses its own environmentality in the cellular language implanted by the poet. At the same time, the material element of Bök's text, namely the organism itself, is granted agency in its ability to "express" or act in its influence on the poem that is produced, a power that can be realized only within the textual space created by the poet.

The ecopoetic implications of the Xenotext are perhaps more evident in one of the poet's more conventional texts. In Bök's Crystallography (2003), he contends that words don't mimic their environment but actually create their own reality, their own space—a textual space. The speaker explains in the book's opening that "A crystal assembles itself out of its own constituent /

disarray" and reiterates that it orients itself only "by chance into its correct location" (2003, 12). The poet's recognition of the random order of a crystal is directly compared to language only a few stanzas later:

> A compound (word) dissolved in a liquid
> supercooled under microgravitational
> conditions precipitates out of solution
> in (alphabetical) order to form crystals
> ...................
> A word is a bit of crystal in formation.
>
> (2003, 12)

Comparing language to chemistry, the speaker claims that words are transformed into something meaningful, something ordered. In a sense, like crystals, words combine randomly to create a structure, an alphabet, which carries meaning. Asserting the parallel between crystalline structure and language, the poet implies that words engage in a living process in which meaning grows and changes based on their counterparts and their environments. The recognition that language takes meaning from its position in its space, relative to its surroundings, is inherently ecopoetic. Although Bök's poetry often lies on the border between poetry and science, his writing constitutes an investigation into language and form that is uniquely suited to an unnatural ecopoetic critique because his challenge to fixed mediums and forms arises from the same inquiry into boundaries between language and biology or, put more broadly, between culture and nature, that lies at the heart of unnatural ecopoetics.

Bök's poetry, like Goldsmith's, elects to engage with new mediums in order to better express the naturalcultural elements of real-world experience in text. While offering different examples, the two poets use unique mediums to move beyond the limitations of language and recognize its multiplicity. In a sense, by reading the unconventional and sometimes extrapoetic work of poets like Bök and Goldsmith through the lens of unnatural ecopoetics, scholars not only draw new types of texts into ecocritical critique but also propel the field away from one of its most restrictive limitations—writing itself. Responding to Morton's charge that writing encounters the "slippery, tricksterish qualities of never quite meaning what it says or saying what it means," unnatural ecopoetics focuses on self-reflexivity and looks to any text, whether extrapoetic or more conventional poetic forms, where language's limitations are recognized and formally foregrounded (2007, 31). Morton identifies a challenge with which ecocriticism has since been contending. He rightly identifies the instability in written representations of nature and, indeed, the risk or trick of its failure.

Morton's proposed solution, which he calls "ecomimesis," aims "to go beyond the aesthetic dimension altogether. It wants to break out of the normative aesthetic frame, go beyond art" (2007, 31). Here, Morton is highlighting the need to recognize the artificiality in representation—not attempting to hide the literary construction, but to foreground it.

Unnatural ecopoetics takes on Morton's charge by recognizing and embracing the artificiality and subjectivity inherent in the writing process. From here, as the previous chapters illustrate, unnatural ecopoetics has the potential to enhance understandings of a variety of texts that do not overtly engage with nature but instead engage deeply with their environmentality. This new lens can be applied even to those pieces that reach beyond the boundaries of the text or the poem into new mediums and genres, which actively participate in their own constructedness, a move that is essential in formulating textual space. Consider, for instance, the drawn poems of Robert Grenier or even more overtly visual forms of expression in the mixed-media work of artists like Patrick Haemmerlein.[2] The challenge to textual fixity that is emphasized in the unnatural ecopoetic readings of chapters 2 and 3 might be further exaggerated in relation to Grenier's drawn poems.

Grenier's poems present unique challenges for poetic critique but new possibilities when approached through the lens of unnatural ecopoetics. The poems lie between visual art and poetry as they employ drawn letters to form lines, each of which is identifiable by its color. Ondrea E. Ackerman considers the materiality of letters themselves and Grenier's emphasis on their constructedness in "Wandering Lines: Robert Grenier's Drawing Poems." She writes, "Grenier's poetry, however strange and unconventional it may be, is about the production of letters out of their material component parts—the physical and visual lines" (2013, 135). As Ackerman argues, much of Grenier's project involves foregrounding the letter as a constructed object and one that brings with it a great deal of subjectivity. In one poem, which the poet himself clarifies for readers in "Drawing Poems/'Rough' Translations," it is clear that Grenier's letters are not easily decipherable and present some challenges for readers in accurately interpreting the poem's content. Only after a great deal of inspection and from familiarity with the poet's handwriting (from analyzing a number of his drawn poems) can one begin to decode the drawn letters and discern the words that make the poem. With the help of the poet himself, we can conclude that his poem reads "MOOER (green), MOOS (red), MOO (blue), AT (black)" (Grenier 2002–4, 7).[3] Once one finally deciphers the words themselves, he or she might question, as Ackerman does, what it means to "moo," what is a "mooer," and what might it "moo / at" (2013, 135). Ultimately, Grenier's foregrounding of the constructedness of words directly informs interpretations of the words themselves. Once the reader has been prompted to question the accuracy and fixity of the words themselves, he or she is forced to consider the authenticity of their meanings or whether they accurately represent their real-world counterpart. In this case, the words are translations of real-world experience (sound) into language, but the textual depiction of the sounds is embellished, revealing its radical dissimilarity to the sound itself and exaggerating the impossibility of an authentic rendering of heard, especially nonhuman, sounds to language. The apparent constructedness of the letters coupled with the obviously inauthentic sound implications of the words reveals a lived experience of the sounds while avoiding what Morton calls the "slippery, tricksterish qualities of never quite meaning what it says or saying what it means." Grenier's poems never claim to stand in for an experience or to express nature, but rather to capture experience in its inauthentic and entirely constructed glory and ensure that readers are aware of the inevitable gap between lived experience and textual renderings of it through the highly mediated textual space of the poem.

The poet's interest in capturing experience is precisely what situates his work for ecopoetic readings. Another series of drawn poems, *For Larry Eigner*,[4] reveals Grenier's struggle with the relationship between lived experience and language and makes it clear how the lens of unnatural ecopoetics offers new possibilities for reading his work. "For Larry Eigner 6," appears to read "moon / letters / page" and includes a red circle with a line through it. One of his most legible drawn poems, "For Larry Eigner 12," appears to read "A Natural / Language / couldn't / be." In both poems, Grenier's self-reflexive language comments on the inevitable distance between language and nature. He clearly distinguishes the physical ("moon") from its translation to language ("letters") and its final placement in text (on the "page") in both the sixth and twelfth poems in the series. In the later poem in the *For Larry Eigner* sequence, though, the poet dismisses the possibility of reconciling the unadulterated physical world with language, implying that language can never be "natural." Moving past the quest for language to express nature, the sequence embraces the immediacy of the moment and the experience in all of its mediated wonder. In "For Larry Eigner 13," the image takes precedence. The poem appears to read "water / at nigh / t." In direct contrast to the previous poem, the thirteenth poem questions the need for language as it turns unequivocally to the image. By making reading difficult, Grenier institutes a self-reflexivity in his texts, which he explains in *Farming the Words: Talking with Robert Grenier*. The poet clarifies the purpose of self-reflexive language when he explains that his hope with his drawn poems is that "nobody can recognize what they are... and then there might be some hope for seeing what's being said as actually happening in the place where it occurs. One thing that might happen in the 'ecopoetics scene,' roughly... is that there might be a reverse projection of the condition of the environment which would emanate from language" (2009, 59). Grenier's suggestion that scholars of ecopoetics might consider how environment "emanate[s] from language" rather than the other way around highlights the textuality of his work. When poetry is revealed for its textual limitations, as it is through the ambiguity of language in Grenier's drawn poems, it ceases to attempt mimesis but instead becomes a site in itself or a textual space.

Reading Grenier's poetry through the lens of unnatural ecopoetics reveals that language and form come together even in extrapoetic texts to create a foregrounded textual space where the naturalcultural elements of environmental experience are exposed, including not only material factors but also the various nonmaterial memories, thoughts, emotions, and distractions that permeate the perceiver's mind. Found poetry is perhaps the most obvious example of where visual poetry is heading in the twenty-first century. *The Found Poetry Review* and other such forums, which are dedicated to foregrounding the poetics of everyday life, demonstrate that poetry is always present in the world and only needs to be properly contextualized in order to be received for its poetic underpinnings.[5] In other areas of visual art, the union of art and everyday life or, to go further, material and nonmaterial facets of experience, is even more pronounced.[6] Visual artist Patrick Haemmerlein, for instance, engages with environment in diverse ways by including not only material elements of space but also the nonmaterial subjective factors that influence the artist.

Haemmerlein gathers objects from his immediate surroundings, namely the streets of Los Angeles, including extratextual references in the form of old books and naturalcultural objects like wood (a perfect union of nature and culture in its natural origins in a tree and its cultural use as construction material) gathered from the region and fuses them into a collage that is framed by his own creative and entirely subjective experience in a particular place and time. One piece, "Your All Just Feathers in My Nest," draws together the prominent images of a bird and flowers with staples of urban life. As the city skyline is blended with traffic lights, airplanes, birds, flowers, and other plants, Haemmerlein's image visually fuses nature and culture. Even more important, perhaps, is the image's frame. Haemmerlein's trademark is the inclusion of book pages to frame his images. Pages from math, music, and literary texts form a collage at the top of the canvas. The artist himself locates his work in his physical experiences, saying, "Your all just feathers in my nest was a tag I saw on the streets of LA. It's just what the Universe provided that day, my artwork works a lot that way, a lot of it is created with luck and chance and things I come across—books, places and, in this case, a street tag" (Haemmerlein). The material space of Los Angeles, including its natural and cultural elements, is literally infused into a creative rendering of the space in a particular moment. In its introduction to his show, The Porch Gallery in Ojai, California, explains Haemmerlein's creative process in detail: "Creating only from photographs he takes, Patrick layers his imagery on found wood & recycled book pages and then applies watercolors to bring the artwork to life" (Porch Gallery 2015). In this sense, his art literally employs its place through its infusion of found objects ranging from wood to street tags, but all the while acknowledges its own artificiality by enhancing the unreality of the photo through watercolors. Choosing to exaggerate his own subjective experience of the scene rather than leaving the seemingly real original image untouched, Haemmerlein foregrounds what I see as a textual space, where his own role as artist is revealed, and subsequently he exposes the influence of nonmaterial elements on the piece, including the artist's thoughts, memories, and emotions. The artist includes the material components of the street tag, wood, and the found pages of prose, sheet music, dictionary definitions, and other texts from all around the world with his nonmaterial influences, ultimately rendering the specific cityscape before him as a visual text that foregrounds a naturalcultural environment.

Unnatural ecopoetics provides a path for analyzing a variety of texts, including visual ones, that incorporate various material and nonmaterial elements of environmentality while recognizing the inability of any text to accurately translate an objective reality to the page. Haemmerlein's work, then, is suitable for unnatural ecopoetic critique despite being visual art because it shows itself cognizant of its own artificiality through its intentionally unreal watercolor scenes. While maintaining the value of local natural and cultural material objects, his work recognizes the ties between the local and the global through the variety of texts employed, and continues to hinge on his own nonmaterial subjective experience. When readers acknowledge how unnatural ecopoetics can enlighten understandings of visual art, both in relation to visual poets like Grenier and overtly visual work, like Haemmerlein's, they can begin to recognize that ecopoetics extends into poetic sentiment, ranging from writing style to visual arts that actively engage with form and language while acknowledging their own inherent constructedness. Just as poetics is not limited to texts organized in rigidly structured lines, ecopoetics is useful in analyzing large swaths of texts, both extrapoetic and more traditional poetic forms.

In reading beyond the specific form of poetry and into other genres that make use of poetic methodologies, unnatural ecopoetics, like poetics more generally, extends beyond traditional poetry. In contemporary poetry, the movement away from the line is evidenced by the rise of prose poetry, found poems, and other highly conceptual poetic gestures that challenge the assumption that poetics is limited to its traditional manifestations. Unnatural ecopoetics encourages readers to consider how environments become present in a wide variety of texts that display poetic sensibilities, including prose. I contend that through this new lens, readers can recognize how textual space functions even in prose in order to express the naturalcultural elements of environmentality.

Vanessa Place's 2008 novel *La Medusa* demonstrates the promise of an unnatural ecopoetic critique of prose. The novel is a literary collage of the voices of Place's many characters—ranging from a conscious corpse to a young girl to a trucker and his wife—with medical definitions, photographs, ink blots, poetry, physical landmarks, literary references, formal intrusions, fairy tales, and screenplay directives. Blatantly disruptive, the novel presents the reader with the challenge of unraveling its many elements and discovering the meaning of its title. While Place's book is a novel, it is poetic in its investment in form and figurative language. Seen through the lens of unnatural ecopoetics, the novel creates a textual space where the naturalcultural material and nonmaterial elements of various experiences of Los Angeles are made active. As various characters present their subjective encounters with the place, the novel's fragmented structure intermingles those facets of experience with the material elements of the city on the page. In the textual space of the novel, the naturalcultural elements of experience are moved to the fore.

To create a textual space, Place foregrounds the constructedness of the text and employs self-reflexive language that emphasizes the distance between words and the reality they purport to express. The novel's textuality is made apparent through constant intrusions in the text, which remind the reader of the formal constructedness of the page. Such moments occur throughout the novel in the author's use of screenplay directives or slug lines, which place particular sections in one character's consciousness and in a specific physical location ("INT. MYLES P.'S SEMI-RTE. 40, OUTSIDE FLAGSTAFF, AZ-DAY," "EXT. JORGE'S HOUSE-OAKWOOD, VENICE-DAY") (Place 2008, 17, 23). These slug lines are used to locate and describe scenes in screenplays, but in Place's novel they not only locate and describe but also initiate the reader into a particular consciousness while simultaneously implying the artificiality of

Hollywood and its robust film culture. The slug lines mark disruptions in the text by indicating shifting perspectives and thus make the reader hyperaware of the text itself. Such awareness is enhanced by the novel's use of formal intrusions, including lines, boxes, and unusual spatial arrangements on the page. The book begins with a six-line "Intro" followed by a dashed line with the words "tear here" below it (Place 2008, 15). A similar line appears just before the "Outro" of the book, indicating that the reader should "detach at perforation" (459). The lines direct the reader to acknowledge the page as paper, which can be cut or torn. In much the same way, Place's continual usage of text boxes, which separate one section of text from another, and atypical spatial arrangements that displace one part of the text or leave white space on the page, demand that the reader acknowledge the constructedness of the text or, put another way, to recognize the text as text.

The formal insistence on the textuality of the novel is aided by the author's juxtaposition of photos of the brain with medical definitions of its parts and diagrams of their particular anatomical locations. There are different iterations of this definition/diagram/photo paradigm throughout the book, beginning with the "Pineal Gland," which "regulates circadian rhythm" and then moving to the "Hippocampus," which is "significant in temporary storage of new declarative (facts/events) memory, not involved in procedural (motor skull/routine) memory; negligible for consciousness; essential for the autobiographical self" (16, 82). Recurring twelve times throughout the novel, these brief moments act self-reflexively as they juxtapose verbal description of how the brain functions with visual images of the organ and scientific maps of where the part is located on the brain.[7] In these moments, the reader becomes distinctly aware of the difference between verbal accounts and visual images. While the definitions describe the brain's functions, they do not reflect the anatomical location or the appearance of the structure in the brain. Words are revealed as distinctly different from reality in these recurring moments. The author's insistence on the constructedness of the text and the limitations of language throughout the novel make *La Medusa* a promising site for unnatural ecopoetic critique because it foregrounds textual space.

With its creation of a textual space, Place's novel demonstrates how material and nonmaterial elements can be revealed and how they can attain the power to express themselves with equal force. When they read through the lens of unnatural ecopoetics, critics realize that *La Medusa* presents the city of Los Angeles both as a physical site with material elements and a nonmaterial idea with its sprawling freeways and endlessly intertwining narratives as a medusa-like space. The material aspects of the city are integrated into the narrative through regular references to popular Los Angeles landmarks and cultural touchstones.[8] However, in an "interior" aside, the city is described as

> a place mostly imagined…with this shore which spreads horizontally like coral fingering the sea. They say there's no center here, but they're wrong about that as well, for Emerson said a city lives by remembering, and if by remembering you mean a constant crop of citizens or the ability to lobby the hearts of any people, then the center of this city is its remembering, and if by remembering you mean the chaptering and concentration of unrelated but adjacent segments, herein lies a constantly remembered center. (Place 2008, 47)

Here, the city is presented as more than its physical or material parts. While it seems to have "no center," the narrator explains that Los Angeles is centered by its ability to pull together "unrelated but adjacent segments" into a "remembered" or perhaps "imagined" center. Like the form of the book itself, the city is constructed from its fragmented or unrelated parts. The material and nonmaterial connect in the unification of these various parts of Los Angeles. In what appears to be another "interior" aside, the narrator identifies culture or nonmaterial elements that center even the centerless material space: "It's a cluster-fuck, this coraled thing, a series of conjoined colonies, a city with no downtown. But as anyone can see, there are template nuclei and patterned knots of thought" (2008, 78). The emergence of a pattern within the decentered city is directly attributable to the textual space, where the material and nonmaterial are exposed.

What is perhaps even more compelling about reading *La Medusa* through the lens of unnatural ecopoetics is that the textual space also grants the material and nonmaterial elements of the city agency. As the "coraled thing" that is the city is implicitly linked to recurring references to "threads of snakes" and a "rat's nest" that displays "form without structure," the book's title character, Medusa, appears to stand in for the city itself (2008, 77, 69).[9] As such, the novel grants the city agency by expressing the material and nonmaterial elements that compose it through the perspectives of a variety of characters that embody the city's diversity. In essence, the city speaks in the novel's textual space, giving voice to the various elements that constitute it.

As the example of *La Medusa* demonstrates, unnatural ecopoetics provides a critical lens that recognizes the foregrounded textual space as a site where the material and nonmaterial elements of environmentality are expressed and made active. Nontraditional poems and extrapoetic texts like those of Grenier,

Bök, Haemmerlein, and Place are only a handful of examples of future directions for unnatural ecopoetics. As critics discover the ecopoetic sentiments that drive the textual and formal play of much contemporary art and writing, this new era of ecopoetic theory opens the door to analyzing a vast array of texts in traditional poetic genres and extrapoetic contexts. Growing from the ecocritical push toward materiality and away from traditional ideas of nature, unnatural ecopoetics presents possibilities for a future of ecopoetics that lies beyond the genre of nature-oriented writing and outside the limited scope of environment as purely physical. Unnatural ecopoetics provides a bridge between ecocriticism's focus on physical environments and a broader interest in how the material and nonmaterial elements of environmental experience come together on the page.

## NOTES

1. Although I focus on Place's novel, *La Medusa*, it is important to note that she straddles the line between poetry and prose and is well known for her poetry. Her work includes the *Tragodía* trilogy, *Dies: A Sentence* (2005), and *Boycott* (2013).

2. Further examples and commentary on Patrick Haemmerlein's work can be found on his blog at http://rural1028.blogspot.com/.

3. Grenier provides a "translation" of some of his poetry in "Drawing Poems/'Rough' Translations."

4. Grenier's *For Larry Eigner* series can be found online in the *Light and Dust Mobile Anthology of Poetry*.

5. For more information, visit www.foundpoetryreview.com.

6. John Scanlan, who considers the important implications of visual art more extensively in *On Garbage*, looks at the work of Joseph Cornell as an example of how visual art can and must embrace its own construction in order to be effective. He contends that in Cornell's work, "a gap is opened that separates art object and reality, artist and world, and it is into this gap that the artist moves in making the object public, and into which the viewer must move in order to make a connection" (Scanlan 2005, 95). The gap that Scanlan identifies within Cornell's work resembles the type of foregrounding of artistic construction along with the union of nature and culture that are fundamental to unnatural ecopoetics.

7. A few of these iterations do not include a diagram of the brain, but only a photo.

8. There are constant references to locations and cultural touchstones within the Los Angeles area, the most prominent of which is Beverly Hills, but there are also specific references to Forest Lawn, the La Brea tar pits, the Los Angeles County Art Museum, Peterson Automotive Museum, the Grapevine, the UCLA Bruins, and Wilshire Boulevard (Place 2008, 88, 211–13).

9. Throughout the book, the concept of the rat's nest recurs in relation to the brain and in reference to chaos, as in Dr. Casper Bowles's surgical removal of "a rat's nest of a tumor" (2008, 69). As the rat's nest is linked to the brain through Casper, the further conflation of the brain with "snakes" implies a connection between the confusion of the rat's nest, the image of entangled snakes, and the myth of Medusa as a figure cursed with a head of vicious snakes.

# Bibliography

Abram, David. 1996. *The Spell of the Sensuous*. New York: Vintage.

Ackerman, Ondrea E. 2013. "Wandering Lines: Robert Grenier's Drawing Poems." *Journal of Modern Literature* 36 (4): 133–53.

Alaimo, Stacy. 2010. *Bodily Natures: Science, Environment, and the Material Self*. Bloomington: Indiana University Press.

Allen, Edward. 2012. "'Visible Earshot': The Returning Voice of Susan Howe." *Cambridge Quarterly* 41 (4): 397–421.

Altieri, Charles. 1998. *Postmodernisms Now: Essays on Contemporaneity in the Arts*. University Park: Pennsylvania State University Press.

Ammons, A. R. 1965. *Corsons Inlet*. Ithaca, NY: Cornell University Press.

———. 1965. *Tape for the Turn of the Year*. Ithaca, NY: Cornell University Press.

———. 1974. *Sphere*. New York: Norton.

———. 1993. *Garbage*. New York: Norton.

———. 1996. *Set in Motion: Essays, Interviews, and Dialogues*. Edited by Zofia Burr. Ann Arbor: University of Michigan Press.

———. 1997. *Glare*. New York: Norton.

Arigo, Christopher. 2008. "Notes Toward an Ecopoetics: Revising the Postmodern Sublime and Juliana Spahr's *This Connection of Everyone with Lungs*." How2 3 (2): 1–20.

Back, Rachel Tzvia. 2002. *Led by Language: The Poetry and Prose of Susan Howe*. Tuscaloosa: University of Alabama Press.

Barad, Karen. 2007. *Meeting the Universe Halfway: Quantum Physics and the Entanglement of Matter and Meaning*. Durham, NC: Duke University Press.

Bate, Jonathan. 2000. *The Song of the Earth*. Cambridge: Harvard University Press.

Bedient, Calvin. 2013. "Against Conceptualism: Defending the Poetry of Affect." *Boston Review* 38 (4): 70–75.

Bennett, Jane. 2010. *Vibrant Matter: A Political Ecology of Things*. Durham, NC: Duke University Press.

Bennett, Robert J. 2011. "Malachy Postlethwayt 1707–67: Genealogy and Influence of an Early Economist and 'Spin Doctor.'" *Genealogists Magazine* 30 (6): 187–94.

Bloom, Harold. 1975. "A. R. Ammons: The Breaking of the Vessels." *Salmagundi* 31/32: 185–203.

———. 2004. *The Art of Reading Poetry*. New York: HarperCollins.

Bök, Christian. 2003. *Crystallography*. Toronto: Coach House.

———. 2005. "A Silly Key: Some Notes on *Soliloquy* by Kenneth Goldsmith." *Open Letter: A Canadian Journal of Writing and Theory* 12 (7): 62–68.

———. 2008. "The Xenotext Experiment." *SCRIPTed* 5 (2): n.p. Web.

Bragard, Véronique. 2013. "Languages of Waste: Matter and Form in our Garb-age." *ISLE: Interdisciplinary Studies in Literature and Environment* 20 (3): 459–63.

Bryson, J. Scott, ed. 2002. *Ecopoetry: A Critical Introduction*. Salt Lake City: University of Utah Press.

Buell, Frederick. 1999. "Ammons's Peripheral Vision: *Tape for the Turn of the Year* and *Garbage*." In Schneider, *Complexities of Motion*, 214–38.

Buell, Lawrence. 2005. *The Future of Environmental Criticism: Environmental Crisis and Literary Imagination*. Malden, MA: Blackwell.

Clark, Hilary. 1991. "The Mnemonics of Autobiography: Lyn Hejinian's *My Life*." *Biography* 14 (4): 315–35.

Clark, Timothy. 2011. *The Cambridge Introduction to Literature and the Environment*. Cambridge: Cambridge University Press.

Costello, Bonnie. 1989. "The Soil and Man's Intelligence: Three Contemporary Landscape Poets." *Contemporary Literature* 30 (3): 412–33.

Dikovitskay, Margaret. 2005. *Visual Culture: The Study of the Visual After the Cultural Turn*. Cambridge, MA: MIT Press.

Durand, Marcella. 2002. "The Ecology of Poetry." *Ecopoetics* 2: 58–62.

Dworkin, Craig. 2005. "Zero Kerning." *Open Letter: A Canadian Journal of Writing and Theory* 12 (7): 10–20.

———. 2011. "The Fate of the Echo." In *Against Expression: An Anthology of Conceptual Writing*, edited by Craig Dworkin and Kenneth Goldsmith, xxiii–xlviii. Evanston, IL: Northwestern University Press.

Dworkin, Craig, and Kenneth Goldsmith, eds. 2011. *Against Expression: An Anthology of Conceptual Writing*. Evanston, IL: Northwestern University Press.

Elder, John. 1996. *Imagining the Earth: Poetry and the Vision of Nature*. 2nd ed. Athens: University of Georgia Press.

Felstiner, John. 2009. *Can Poetry Save the Earth?: A Field Guide to Nature Poems*. New Haven, CT: Yale University Press.

Fisher-Wirth, Ann, and Laura-Gray Street. 2013. *The Ecopoetry Anthology*. San Antonio, TX: Trinity University Press.

Fletcher, Angus. 2004. *A New Theory for American Poetry*. Cambridge: Harvard University Press.

Foster, Hal. 1986. "Subversive Signs." *Recodings: Art, Spectacle, Cultural Politics*. Seattle: Bay Press.

Fredman, Stephen. 1990. *Poet's Prose: The Crisis in American Verse*. 2nd ed. Cambridge: Cambridge University Press.

Gander, Forrest. 2006–9. "The Future of the Past: The Carboniferous and Eco-Poetics." *Ecopoetics* 6/7: 169–73.

Garner, Dwight. 2013. "The Words We Heard as Horrors Sank In: 'Seven American Deaths and Disasters' Transcribes the News." *New York Times*, June 19, C1.

Gifford, Terry. 1995. *Green Voices: Understanding Contemporary Nature Poetry*. Manchester: Manchester University Press.

Goldman, Judith. 2011. "Re-thinking 'Non-retinal Literature': Citation, 'Radical Mimesis,' and Phenomenologies of Reading in Conceptual Writing." *Postmodern Culture* 22 (1): n.p.

Goldsmith, Kenneth. 2000. *Fidget*. Toronto: Coach House Books.

———. 2001. *Soliloquy*. New York: Granary Books.

———. 2003. *Day*. Great Barrington, MA: The Figures.

———. 2004. "Being Boring." The First Séance for Experimental Literature. Los Angeles: Disney REDCAT Theatre. November.

———. 2005. *The Weather*. Los Angeles: Make Now.

———. 2007. *Traffic*. Los Angeles: Make Now.

———. 2008. *Sports*. Los Angeles: Make Now.

———. 2011. *Uncreative Writing: Managing Language in the Digital Age*. New York: Columbia University Press.

———. 2013. *Seven American Deaths and Disasters*. Brooklyn, NY: PowerHouse.

Gooch, Brad. 1993. *City Poet: The Life and Times of Frank O'Hara*. New York: Knopf.

Grenier, Robert. 1997. *For Larry Eigner*. Light and Dust Mobile Anthology of Poetry. Edited by Karl Young. http://www.thing.net/~grist/l&d/grenier/lgloo.htm.

———. 2002–4. "Drawing Poems/'Rough' Translations." *Robert Grenier* (EPC author home page). Web. http://epc.buffalo.edu/authors/grenier/.

———. 2009. "AFTER / NOON / SUN / SHINE." *Area Sneaks* 2: n.p.

Grenier, Robert, Timothy Shaner, Jonathan Skinner, and Isabelle Pelissier. 2009. *Farming the Words: Talking with Robert Grenier*. Bowdoinham, ME: Field Books.

Grubbs, David, and Susan Howe. 2011. *Frolic Architecture*. Blue Chopsticks. CD.

Haemmerlein, Patrick. N.d. "Your All Just Feathers in My Nest." Mixed media. Porch Gallery, Ojai, CA.

Haraway, Donna. 2000. *How Like a Leaf: An Interview with Thyrza Nichols Goodeve*. London: Routledge. First published 1998.

Heise, Ursula K. 2008. *Sense of Place, Sense of Planet: The Environmental Imagination of the Global*. Oxford: Oxford University Press.

Hejinian, Lyn. (1978) 1996. *Writing Is an Aid to Memory*. Los Angeles: Sun and Moon Press.

———. 2000. *Happily*. Sausalito, CA: Post-Apollo Press.

———. 2000. *The Language of Inquiry*. Berkeley: University of California Press.

——. 2002. *My Life*. København: Green Integer.

——. 2003. *My Life in the Nineties*. New York: Shark Books.

Hick, Darren Hudson. 2010. "Forgery and Appropriation in Art." *Philosophy Compass* 5 (12): 1047–56.

Howe, Susan. 1990. *Singularities*. Middletown, CT: Wesleyan University Press.

——. 2003. *The Midnight*. New York: New Directions.

——. 2010. *That This*. New York: New Directions.

Huntsperger, David. 2010. *Procedural Form in Postmodern American Poetry: Berrigan, Antin, Silliman, and Hejinian*. New York: Palgrave Macmillan.

Iijima, Brenda. 2010. *The Ecolanguage Reader*. Brooklyn, NY: Portable Press at Yo-Yo Labs.

Iovino, Serenella, and Serpil Oppermann. 2012. "Theorizing Material Ecocriticism: A Diptych." *ISLE: Interdisciplinary Studies in Literature and Environment* 19 (3): 448–75.

——. 2014. *Material Ecocriticism*. Bloomington: Indiana University Press.

Izenberg, Oren. 2003. "Language Poetry and Collective Life." *Critical Inquiry* 30 (1): 132–59.

Kaufmann, Michael. 1994. *Textual Bodies: Modernism, Postmodernism, and Print*. Lewisburg, PA: Bucknell University Press.

Keats, John. 1917. *Endymion. Poems: Endymion. The Volume of 1820 and Other Poems*, edited by W. T. Young, 5–140. Cambridge: Cambridge University Press.

Keller, Lynn. 1995. "An Interview with Susan Howe." *Contemporary Literature* 36 (1): 1–34.

——. 2012. "Beyond Imagining, Imagining Beyond." *PMLA* 127 (3): 579–85.

Knickerbocker, Scott. 2012. *Ecopoetics: The Language of Nature, the Nature of Language*. Amherst: University of Massachusetts Press.

"Landfills: Frequently Asked Questions." 2013. *DHEC* (South Carolina Department of Health and Environmental Control). March.

Lefebvre, Henri. 1991. *The Production of Space*. Translated by Donald Nicholson-Smith. Malden, MA: Blackwell.

Linstrom, John. 2011. "Seeking a Center for Ecopoetics." *Valparaiso Poetry Review* 12 (2): n.p.

Lynes, Katherine R. 2009. "'Sprung from American Soil': The 'Nature' of Africa in the Poetry of Helene Johnson." *ISLE: Interdisciplinary Studies in Literature and Environment* 16 (3): 525–49.

Magi, Jill. 2010. "Ecopoetics and the Adversarial Consciousness: Challenges to Nature Writing, Environmentalism, and Notions of Individual Agency." *The Ecolanguage Reader*, edited by Brenda Iijima, 237–52. Brooklyn, NY: Portable Press at Yo-Yo Labs.

Morrison, Susan Signe. 2013. "Waste Aesthetics: Form as Restitution." *ISLE: Interdisciplinary Studies in Literature and Environment* 20 (3): 464–78.

———. 2015. *The Literature of Waste: Material Ecopoetics and Ethical Matter*. New York: Palgrave Macmillan.

Morton, Timothy. 2007. *Ecology Without Nature: Rethinking Environmental Aesthetics*. Cambridge: Harvard University Press.

Naylor, Paul. 1999. *Poetic Investigations: Singing the Holes in History*. Evanston, IL: Northwestern University Press.

*New Englander and Yale Review*. 1889. 51.232.

O'Hara, Frank. 1964. *Lunch Poems*. San Francisco: City Lights.

———. 1971. *The Collected Poems of Frank O'Hara. Berkeley*: University of California Press.

Perelman, Bob. 1985. *Writing/Talks*. Carbondale: Southern Illinois University Press.

———. 1996. *The Marginalization of Poetry: Language Writing and Literary History*. Princeton, NJ: Princeton University Press.

Perloff, Marjorie. 1985. *The Dance of the Intellect: Studies in the Poetry of the Pound Tradition*. Cambridge: Cambridge University Press.

———. 1991. *Radical Artifice: Writing Poetry in the Age of Media*. Chicago: University of Chicago Press.

———. 1999. "How a Thing Will / Unfold": Fractal Rhythms in A. R. Ammons's *Briefings*." In Schneider, *Complexities of Motion*, 68–82.

———. 2005. "'Moving Information': On Kenneth Goldsmith's *The Weather*." *Open Letter: A Canadian Journal of Writing and Theory* 12 (7): 75–85.

———. 2010. *Unoriginal Genius: Poetry by Other Means in the New Century*. Chicago: University of Chicago Press.

Place, Vanessa. 2008. *La Medusa*. Tuscaloosa: University of Alabama Press.

———. 2011. *Tragodia 1: Statement of Facts*. Los Angeles: Insert Blanc.

Place, Vanessa, and Robert Fitterman. 2009. *Notes on Conceptualisms*. Brooklyn, NY: Ugly Duckling Presse.

Porch Gallery, Ojai. 2015. http://porchgalleryojai.com/patrick-haemmerlein-just -feathers-nest/.

Quartermain, Peter. 1992. *Disjunctive Poetics: From Gertrude Stein and Louis Zukofsky to Susan Howe*. Cambridge: Cambridge University Press.

Quetchenbach, Bernard W. 2000. *Back from the Far Field: American Nature Poetry in the Late Twentieth Century*. Charlottesville: University Press of Virginia.

Randall, Marilyn. 2007. "Recycling Recycling or *plus ça change…*." *Other Voices* 3 (1): n.p.

Rasula, Jed. 1987. "The Politics of, the Politics In." In *Politics and Poetic Value*, edited by Robert von Hallberg, 315–22. Chicago: University of Chicago Press.

———. 2002. *This Compost: Ecological Imperatives in American Poetry*. Athens: University of Georgia Press.

Reinfeld, Linda. 1992. *Language Poetry: Writing as Rescue*. Baton Rouge: Louisiana State University Press.

Reznikoff, Charles. 1978. *Testimony*. Los Angeles: Black Sparrow.

Rich, Motoko. 2008. "Literacy Debate: Online, R U Really Reading?" *New York Times*, July 27.

Scanlan, John. 2005. *On Garbage*. London: Reaktion.

Schmidt, Christopher. 2008. "The Waste-Management Poetics of Kenneth Goldsmith." *SubStance* 37 (2): 25–40.

———. 2014. *The Poetics of Waste: Queer Excess in Stein, Ashbery, Schuyler, and Goldsmith*. New York: Palgrave Macmillan.

Schneider, Stephen P. 1994. *A. R. Ammons and the Poetics of Widening Scope*. Rutherford, NJ: Fairleigh Dickinson University Press.

———, ed. 1999. *Complexities of Motion: New Essays on A. R. Ammons's Long Poems*. Madison, NJ: Fairleigh Dickinson University Press.

Schuster, Joshua. 2005. "On Kenneth Goldsmith: The Avant-Garde at a Standstill." *Open Letter: A Canadian Journal of Writing and Theory* 12 (7): 102–9.

Schwartzburg, Molly. 2005. "Encyclopedic Novelties: On Kenneth Goldsmith's Tomes." *Open Letter: A Canadian Journal of Writing and Theory* 12 (7): 21–35.

Scigaj, Leonard M. 1999. *Sustainable Poetry: Four American Ecopoets*. Lexington: University Press of Kentucky.

Simpson, Megan. 2000. *Poetic Epistemologies: Gender and Knowing in Women's Language-Oriented Writing*. Albany: State University of New York Press.

Skinner, Jonathan. 2001. "Editor's Statement." *Ecopoetics* 1: 5–8.

Slovic, Scott. 2010. "The Third Wave of Ecocriticism: North American Reflections on the Current Phase of the Discipline." *Ecozon@* 1 (1): 4–10.

———. 2012. "Editor's Note." *ISLE: Interdisciplinary Studies in Literature and Environment* 19 (4): 619–21.

Soja, Edward W. 1996. *Thirdspace: Journeys to Los Angeles and Other Real-and-Imagined Places*. Malden, MA: Blackwell.

Spahr, Juliana. 2001. *Everybody's Autonomy: Collective Reading and Collective Identity*. Tuscaloosa: University of Alabama Press.

Spiegelman, Willard. 1999. "Building Up and Breaking Down: The Poetics of Composting." In Schneider, *Complexities of Motion*, 51–67.

Sprague, Jane. 2008. "Ecopoetics: Drawing on the Calfskin Vellum." *How2* 3 (2): 1–11.

Stevens, Wallace. 1997. *Wallace Stevens: Collected Poetry and Prose*. Compiled by Frank Kermode and Joan Richardson. New York: Library of America.

Tobin, Daniel. 1999. "A. R. Ammons and the Poetics of Chaos." In Schneider, *Complexities of Motion*, 113–37.

"Today's Front Pages: Wednesday, September 12, 2001." *Newseum*. http://www.newseum.org/todaysfrontpages/default_archive.asp?fpArchive=091201.

Vendler, Helen. 1999. "*The Snow Poems* and *Garbage*: Episodes in an Evolving Poetics." In Schneider, *Complexities of Motion*, 23–50.

Voros, Gyorgyi. 2000. "Wallace Stevens and A. R. Ammons as Men on the Dump." *Wallace Stevens Journal* 24 (2): 161–75.

———. 2002. "Earth's Echo: Answering Nature in Ammons's Poetry." *Ecopoetry: A Critical Introduction*, edited by J. Scott Bryson, 88–100. Salt Lake City: University of Utah Press.

Weiner, Lawrence. 1978. "Regarding the (A) Use of Language within the Context of Art." *L=A=N=G=U=A=G=E Magazine* 1: 8.

White, Jenny L. 2006. "The Landscapes of Susan Howe's 'Thorow.'" *Contemporary Literature* 47 (2): 236–60.

Zawacki, Andrew. 2012. "Ego and Eco: Saying 'I' in *Expressions of Sea Level*." *Chicago Review* 57 (1–2): 49–62.

# About the Author

SARAH NOLAN is a lecturer at the University of Nevada, Reno. She specializes in American poetry and contemporary literature, with a particular emphasis on ecocriticism and ecopoetics. Nolan has a PhD in English from The University of Nevada, Reno, and received her MA at California State University, Long Beach. In publications in journals ranging from *Studies in American Culture* to *Green Letters: Studies in Ecocriticism* and a variety of essay collections, including *New International Voices in Ecocriticism*, Nolan has explored new directions in ecopoetics. In her current research, she is examining how the poetry of American prisons engages with the environments of incarceration. Currently, she lives in Reno, Nevada, with her husband and two children.

# Index

"A. R. Ammons: The Breaking of the Vessels" (Bloom), 28

Abram, David, 13

Ackerman, Ondrea E., 128

"Against Conceptualization" (Bedient), 100

Alaimo, Stacy, 13–14

Allen, Edward, 77

Altieri, Charles, 48

ambient poetics, theory of, 7–8

Ammons, A. R.: *Garbage* in the poetic development of, 25–27 (*see also* Garbage); traditional approaches to, 27–33. *See also* "Corsons Inlet"

"Ammons's Peripheral Vision" (Buell), 31–32

appropriation poetry: Goldsmith's (eco) poetics, 103–18; history, theories, and criticisms of, 98–103. *See also* conceptual poetry; Seven American Deaths and Disasters

Arigo, Christopher, 8

*Articulation of Sound Forms in Time* (Knickerbocker), 75

artifice, 16

autobiography: Hejinian's *My Life* and, 58–59, 62–64, 69

Back, Rachel Tzvia, 74, 89

Barad, Karen, 71n7

Bate, Jonathan, 6, 10

Bedient, Calvin, 100

"Being Boring" (Goldsmith), 103

Benjamin, Walter, 101

Bennett, Jane, 13, 88, 124

Bennett, Louie, 84, 88

Bernstein, Charles, 101

"Beyond Imagining, Imagining Beyond" (Keller), 124

biocentrism: *Garbage* and, 31–32

Bloom, Harold, 27, 28, 45n3, 118

*Bodily Natures* (Alaimo), 13–14

Bök, Christian, 21, 104, 105, 125–27

Bragard, Véronique, 45n2

Bryson, J. Scott, 6, 22n12, 46n5

Buell, Frederick, 31–32

Buell, Lawrence, 6, 23n15

"Building Up and Breaking Down" (Spiegelman), 31

*Cambridge Companion to Literature and the Environment, The* (Clark), 9

Carson, Anne, 101

Clark, Hilary, 59

Clark, Timothy, 9

colons: in *Garbage*, 35–46

conceptual poetry: defined, 24n27; found poetry of Patrick Haemmerlein, 130–31; Goldsmith's *Seven American Deaths and Disasters* and, 97–98 (*see also* Seven American Deaths and Disasters); history,